Do YOU love Jesus?

God wants you as His family, His friend, and His partner in saving mankind.

Wyveta Kirk

Thanks for being a friend

Dr. Wyveta Kirk

Christian Psychologist

This book is not intended to replace the Holy Bible. Readers should study the Scriptures and ensure that all they read or hear taught is what God's Word says, not blindly accept another's word as accurate. For assistance in handling struggles with spiritual concerns, turning to God in prayer and reading His Word should be the first source one seeks.

Dr. Wyveta Kirk / SuccesSteps Publishing

Do You Love Jesus?/ Dr. Wyveta Kirk – 1st edition.

Print ISBN: 978-0-9971904-4-1

This book is dedicated to believers who at times have doubts of God loving them, question their salvation, or even wonder if God exists, but who deeply want to trust the Lord and to know they are heaven bound. May this book increase your faith and love for all Jesus has done for you since the beginning of time and continues doing for you each day. May you realizing how God has cared for people throughout the ages show you that He will continue caring for you and leave you knowing He has a place in heaven prepared just for you.

The use of the word man and mankind is used to include both genders, and it makes easier writing and reading than using he/she or him/her.

In many provided Scriptures, some words are in bold. If you read the bold words several times, you find they contain the essence of the verse's meaning, and with several readings of the bold words, you remember longer the meaning of the Scripture.

CONTENTS

WHY YOU WERE CREATED

W hen I was four or five years old, my playmate showed me pictures of Bible stories she had colored and asked why we didn't go to church. I began asking to go. Mother agreed, and for months we attended several places. After each Sunday's sermon, Mother studied her Bible for hours. She often said, "We are not going back there. They are not doing what God says," or "They teach things that aren't in the Bible." Finally, she found one where she could find no disagreement. Mother was baptized, and afterwards, we attended worship faithfully. Mother, until she died, and I still attend. Daddy attended sporadically. Yet, in my numerous years of sitting in church pews, many of the concepts in this book are things I never learned nor heard taught. I find it sad, that I have read so many Scriptures and never put it all together to understand how long God had a plan for saving us and for rewarding our efforts for helping others.

A learning was that before our world was made, heaven's Godhead: God the Father, God the Son, and God the Holy Spirit designed a plan for having people join Them and Their thousands of angels as part of Their heavenly family. Before the Garden of Eden was created in preparation for man (Gal.

3:17-22), the Godhead wanted humans They could love and who would bring glory and honor to the Father (Isa. 43: 6-7). Paul describes it this way: *We speak of God's secret wisdom, a wisdom that has been hidden and that **God destined for our glory before time began*** (1Cor. 2:7 my emphasis). Paul told Titus that God promised mankind eternal life before the beginning of time (Tit. 1:2). Each individual person was wanted, known, and loved before the creation of time and our universe. Thank about that for a moment: the God who made heaven and our universe wanted you to live with Him forever.

The Godhead wanted the beings They created to return Their love because of how well cared for they were. The only way to ensure mankind's love was genuine was to allow them the option of not loving. Instead of controlling people and forcing them to love, They made people capable of self-control and allowed them free will. This gave people freedom to choose. Mankind could love the Lord and others, or they could decide to ignore God and others' needs and live as selfishly self-centered as they wanted. However, God offered mankind special promises for obedience and punishment for disobedience.

Jesus provided a definition of love He uses to determine if mankind obeys as is needed for living with Them in Their heavenly home. *Anyone who loves Me will obey My teaching.*

My Father will love them, and We will come to them and make Our home with them. **Anyone who does not love Me will not obey** *My teaching. These words are not My own; they belong to the Father who sent Me* (Jn.14:23-24 my emphasis). Jesus spoke only what His Father wanted said: *I did not speak on My own, but the Father who sent Me commanded Me what to say and how to say all that I have spoken* (Jn. 12:49). Jesus promised if we love Him and keep His commands that He will ask His Father to send the Spirit of truth to live with us and be in us (Jn. 12:15-17). The Holy Spirit helps us remain faithful.

The human beings who commit to obeying the Lord's commands become God's chosen children. **Before creation of the world** God decided He wanted obedient humans to live with Him in eternity (Eph. 1:4 my emphasis). The Father predestined that faithful believers would be adopted as His children through Jesus Christ, in accordance with His pleasure and will (Eph.1:5; Ro. 8:23; Gal. 4:4-7). This was to the praise of His glorious grace, which He has freely given us in the One He loves (Gal.4: 5).

Mankind was created to return the Godhead's love and spend eternity with them

However, from the beginning, men have run from God, disobeyed, and rebelled, while He continued working to have them want to return to Him. God's goal is to lose no one, but He refuses to control men or force their obedience.

The Godhead had to ensure that heaven remained a place where everyone is holy. No sin could be allowed for God cannot look on wickedness (Hab. 1:13). Scripture explains how even angels who sinned were removed from heaven (2 Pe. 2:4; Rev. 12:9, 20:2). As the sinful people we are (Ro. 6:23), no man is worthy of being in the presence of God.

Yet, while the holy Godhead cannot permit sin in their heavenly Paradise, God wants no one to be lost (2 Pe. 3:9). He wants even the worst of sinners to change and live saved. Therefore, in order to allow people the option of being unfaithful, the plan had to include a way to save those who disobeyed and rebelled but then realized their need to change and does so. This required a way to have man be forgiven for doing wrong.

God the Father determined such forgiveness would require a blood sacrifice. He decided blood could pay the debt owed for mankind's sins and leave men holy enough to live in heaven. The Father chose us in Him before the creation of the world and a blood sacrifice was how we could become holy and blameless in His sight (Eph. 1:4). The decision was to have God the Son come to earth, live as a human, and be called Jesus Christ and Son of Man. He would pay the blood price

4

mankind owes for their sins. Once the design for this heavenly plan was completed, our world, our universe, was created by God the Son and the Holy Spirit.

In the beginning God (the Son, the Word) created the heavens and the earth (Ge. 1:1; Ps. 33:6-11), and the Spirit of God hovered over the waters (v.2). The waters stood above the mountains, but at His rebuke the waters fled (Ps. 104:5-7). When we think of how beautiful our planet is with its turquoise waters, snow peaked mountains, colorful flowers, and striking sunsets, we can only imagine how spectacular Jesus has made heaven. Psalm 104 provides a beautiful story of how God formed our earth. This was such an exciting feat that when the foundation of the earth was created, all the angels of God shouted for joy (Job. 38:7). *The earth is the Lord's and everything in it, the world and all who live in it; for He founded it upon the seas and upon the water* (Ps. 24:1-2); *the foundations of the earth and the heavens are the work of Your hands* (Ps. 102:25).

Once everything was perfect for the entrance of mankind, man and woman were created. God created man in His own image; male and female He created them (Ge. 1: 27). God blessed them (v.28) and saw all that He had made was good (v.31).

Scriptures tell us that the God who created all things was the Word, or God the Son, who later would be called Jesus

Christ. Paul tells us that by Jesus all things were created: things in heaven and on earth, visible and invisible (Col. 1:16). John (1:1-4) explains: *In the beginning was the Word (Jesus Christ-the Son), and the Word was with God (the Father), and the Word was God. He was with God in the beginning. Through Jesus all things were made; without Him nothing was made that has been made. In Him was life, and that life was the Light of men.* All things were created by Jesus' spoken Word. Note that John's message shows that the Word was eternal and present from the beginning. God (the Father) made all things through Jesus. Jesus was heaven's creative spokesperson and the one to relate to mankind, carrying out His Father's will. The Son is the radiance of the Father's glory and **the exact representation of the Father's being,** sustaining all things by His powerful Word (Heb. 1:3 my emphasis).

Everything was **created** by Jesus and **for Him**. In Him all things hold together. We are God's workmanship, **created in Christ Jesus to do good works,** which God prepared in advance for us to do (Eph. 2:10 my emphasis). God gives each of us special talents and opportunities for helping others and wants us crediting the Father for our ability to do good deeds (Isa. 43:6-7). We are to glorify the Father in everything we say and do so others want to know Him and spend eternity with the holy Godhead.

God the Father had all His fullness dwell in Jesus, and though Jesus, the Father reconciled to Himself all things on earth or in heaven (Col. 1:16-19). Things were completed exactly as God the Father wanted. The Father put everything and everyone under Jesus' control and made all to be in subjection to Him.

God declared He would do nothing without first revealing it to His servants, the prophets (Amos. 3:7). Old Testament prophets carried messages that God wanted the people to hear. Some concerned events soon to happen; others declared things to happen in the future, including telling of the coming of Christ to earth. Paul called the proclamation of Jesus Christ a mystery hidden for ages long past, but revealed through Old Testament prophetic writings at the command of God so all nations would believe and obey Him (Ro. 16:25-26). Throughout the New Testament, God reminds that all He has done, is doing and will do is in accordance with the Old Testament Scriptures. Harmony of both Testaments reveals the Godhead's plan for redeeming and glorifying mankind. One of the most prophetic pictures is outlined for us in the Jewish feasts found in Leviticus 23, and how centuries later, Jesus Christ changed the feasts' meaning. God now speaks to us by His Son, whom He appointed heir of all things and through whom He made the universe (Heb. 1:2).

When the time had fully come, the divine plan was ready for mankind's redemption. The Word became flesh and made His dwelling among us. Jesus the Word stepped aside from His equality in the Godhead and became subject to the Father by coming to earth and living with other humans. Jesus said, *"Sacrifice and offering You did not desire, but a body You prepared for Me. I have come to do Your will, O God"* (Heb. 10:5-7). God sent His Son, born of woman, to redeem those under law that mankind might receive the full rights of son-ship. The Word became flesh through Mary's womb by the Holy Spirit and the power of the Most High, so the Holy One to be born would also be called the Son of God (Lk. 1:35). On earth, He was named Jesus and called the Christ and Son of Man.

The Godhead's heavenly commitments offered mankind a way to have permanent forgiveness of their sins so men could live eternally with Them in heaven (Eph. 1:4). God the Father based this eternal promise on the willingness of Jesus Christ to offer His blood as payment for the debt men owed for their sins (Jn. 10:18; Heb. 7:27; 9:14). With Jesus' willing agreement, God the Father kept His promise to send His Son into the world to die in man's place (Jn. 3:16; 17:18). He did this so that whoever believed in Jesus should not perish but have eternal life (Jn. 3:16), and who, with help from the Holy Spirit could remain faithful. The Father did not send His Son into the world to condemn the world, but to save the world through Him. He came to save every individual who believes and obeys.

The plan designed by the Father, Son, and Holy Spirit was for all people who live by the Truth of His Word, come into Jesus' Light to know what Jesus has done for them, and what is being done for them through the Father (Jn.1:12-13) and the Holy Spirit (Jn. 16:13-15). Jesus' mission was to bring glory to the Father by saving people to live with them forever (Jn. 14:13). What we know about the Father is revealed in Jesus (Col. 2:9). The Godhead wanted men to realize they can be free from Satan's power that keeps men trapped in sin, and so thoughts of their own death are no longer a dreaded and fearful thing (Heb. 2:14). With Jesus sacrificing His blood on the cross, all men can choose to live assured of having eternal joy in heaven.

When God wanted to do a work on earth that fostered mankind being saved, He found a specific man with whom He knew would obey, such as Moses and Abraham, and made Covenants with them. This moved creation towards the time when Jesus would come to earth. The Covenants with such men included a descendant or seed, and the Seed referred to Jesus coming through their blood line. Scripture does not say 'to seeds,' meaning many people, but 'to your seed,' meaning one person -- who is Christ" (Gal. 3:16). This heavenly inheritance relied on men's faith and God's grace.

Jesus Christ fulfilled men's blood obligations for their sins so fellowship between God and men could last throughout eternity. Men becomes sons of God through faith in Christ Jesus, and being baptized. With baptism, they are clothed with Christ and belong to Christ. Belonging to Christ makes one of Abraham's seed and an heir to the promise of eternity with Him (Gal. 3:26-29). God created Covenants with the Israelites so men would realize the degree of their sins, recognize their need for a Savior, and know that Jesus Christ is the only solution for having their sins permanently forgiven. This lets mankind appreciate the greatness of God's grace.

Without anticipation of men desiring the New Covenant's promise, God could not have endured all the sinful people from Adam and Eve through today. Without heaven's plan pointing to the Messiah, Jesus Christ, and the Old Testament's events that lead to Him, mankind would have ended in the Garden of Eden. God could not have tolerated so much sinfulness. Only the joy of knowing that once Jesus returns again, many glorified sons and daughters will expand heaven's family made it bearable (Heb. 2:10). We know from Jesus' comment that in His Father's house are **many** mansions, and the Father wanted Their plan to have a huge number of people live eternally with Them.

The Godhead's agreement made in heaven was ratified/confirmed with Jesus Christ's death. When, on the cross, Christ said, *"It is finished"* His part of the Father-Son-Spirit heavenly plan was satisfied. Christ's death consummated the divine agreement made in heaven millenniums earlier.

Jesus' death proved He was human; His resurrection proved He was God. When the Father resurrected Christ from the dead, the Father glorified Him by putting Jesus at His right hand in heaven. Jesus Christ's resurrection proved the Father accepted Christ's blood sacrifice for mankind. This completed the Father's part in the divine plan. The Godhead had done their share to allow men to live in heaven. Mankind spending eternity with Them was now dependent upon man's choices. Whether mankind suffers the consequences of God's wrath or the benefits of His love depends on man's response to Jesus' commands.

Jesus will return to judge all people. Then faithful believers will be made new and live in heaven as God's holy family, as the Father, Son, and Spirit wanted before the beginning of all things. It is now up to mankind to fulfill their Covenant obligation.

We humans are made in God's image, and as such, were given a desire to have another to love. Just as many barren women pray nightly on tear-soaked pillows wanting to have a child, God yearns to have more faithful children He can adopt and love. Like the many parents of troublesome, rebellious teenagers who pray their children will change and respond in loving obedience, God longs for us to repent of our sinful ways and return His love. When we change, He promises to make our eternal, heavenly reward better than anything we can imagine or dream. Scripture assures us that no mind has conceived what God has prepared for those who love Him (1 Cor. 2:9). *From the beginning* **God chose you to be saved** *through the sanctifying work of the Spirit and belief in the truth* (2 Th. 2:13). You and I were created to be saved, live forever in heaven as part of the Holy Godhead's family, and share in Their love.

GOD OF THE OLD TESTAMENT

S ome people view God as if He has a split personality. They
see Him as a harsh punisher of wrongs during Old
Testament days and a loving forgiver of sins in New
Testament times. I have heard some say they love Jesus but
not the God who cared for the Israelites. I fear people speak of
such disconnect because, they don't want to face justice for
their sins, and think with Jesus, they won't be held
accountable like the rebellious Israelites were. If they can
make the Father a bad god and Jesus an all loving, forgiving
god, they create a false safety net for themselves. How wrong
they are, and what an eternal price it can cost them. In their
thoughts, they have created a false idol to worship, and it was
likely with Satan's assistance.

However, I understand this disconnect. For years I didn't
know it was God the Son, second person of the Trinity, who
addressed people in the Old Testament and not the Father.
Perhaps that was due to Jesus being called so many names:
Jesus, Christ, God, the Word, Lord, Only Son, an angel, Savior,
Master, Good Shepherd, Teacher, and Son of Man once He
came to earth. Regardless of the name, Jesus is the one who
communicated with people at all times, saying, and doing His

Father's will on earth. God the Son is the one who addressed people in both the Old Testament and New Testament, not God the Father. What the Father wanted said or done, was spoken and completed by Jesus the Word.

We know it was not the Father because Jesus said it wasn't. Jesus told the people of His day that no man has heard His Father's voice nor seen His Father's form (Jn. 5:37). This is such an important point, let me repeat it: Jesus said the Father has never spoken to a human nor been seen by a human. This message is repeated by Timothy (1 Tim. 6:16), and three times John emphasizes that no one but Jesus has ever seen the Father (1:18; 6:46; 1 Jn. 4:12).

Jesus said the Father has never spoken to nor been seen by a human

Perhaps what's confusing is we know when Jesus was baptized, He saw the Spirit of God descend like a dove, and He heard a voice from heaven say, *"This is my Son, whom I love; with Him I am well pleased."* While all present saw a dove, the voice spoke directly and personally to Jesus. When a voice came from heaven and said to Jesus, *"I have glorified it, and will glorify it again"* (Jn. 12:28), the people thought they heard thunder and others an angel. When John heard a voice from the throne of God, he described hearing what sounded like a great multitude, rushing water, and thunder (Rev. 19: 6).

When the three apostles were with Jesus on the mountain, they heard a voice as of a cloud (Lk. 9:35). Scriptures reveal what was said in these examples because the Holy Spirit guided men to write what the Father wanted written for our learning (2 Pe. 1:21), just as He did the many other Bible stories.

While Jesus told people, they have never heard the Father's voice nor seen His form, He added that He is the *only one* who has seen the Father (Jn. 6:46). Jesus made the Father known (Jn. 1:18b). In Christ, all the fullness of the Deity lives in bodily form (Col. 2:9). Therefore, we know what the Father is like by learning what Jesus is like. Jesus said, *"He who has seen Me has seen the Father"* (Jn. 14:9). When Philip asked Jesus to show them the Father, Jesus told him that He is in the Father and the Father is in Him (Jn. 14:8-10). They are so perfectly united, they always think and act alike. To see One was to see Both, because the Son is the radiance of God's glory and the exact representation of His Father's being (Heb. 1:3). The Father did not interact with people because as Jesus said, *"It is the Father living in Me, who is doing His work."* Jesus did and said to men all the Father wanted done (Jn. 14:10).

To love Jesus is to love the Father because they are united so perfectly, they always think and act alike

Places in Old Testament Scriptures (Exe. 20:20) are interpreted as Yahweh, and some take that to mean it is talking about the Father. However, a majority of Bible versions call God of the Old Testament and God of the New Testament the same: Jesus Christ, who is the same yesterday, today, and tomorrow (Heb. 13:8). According to Ligonier.org, this is explained by the early Greek version of the Old Testament, called the Septuagint. It translates the Hebrew word as *Yahweh* and *Adonai* as *kurios*. Yahweh is the revealed name of God in Hebrew and Adonai is one of His titles, often used as *Kurios* or *Lord* in the Septuagint. Because Jews considered God's name too holy to be spoken, they used the title of *Adonai,* or *Kurios,* or Lord. This same title is also quoted throughout the New Testament as one who is absolutely sovereign and conveys divine power and sovereignty and it confirms Jesus' identity. Paul discusses the humiliation and exaltation of God the Son, calling Jesus Lord in the highest sense because of His perfect obedience, death for our sin, and His resurrection that makes Jesus worthy as Lord of all.

Jesus came to earth to reveal His Father to mankind (Mt. 11:27). Jesus was directing mankind according to His Father's will in the Old Testament, just as He continued in the New

Testament. Let me provide a few examples. When Adam walked in the Garden, the LORD asked him, "Where are you?" Adam clearly heard the voice and answered (Ge. 3:9-10). The voice he heard could not have been the Father, because Jesus stated that no man has heard His Father's voice. Therefore, Adam heard God the Son, Jesus' speaking. The Lord Jesus spoke to Moses, as a man speaks to a friend (Ex. 33:11), and He called to Abraham to stop him from sacrificing his son Isaac (Ge. 22:1-18).

At the burning bush, God told Moses to tell the people that I AM had spoken to him, and in the New Testament Jesus uses *I am* multiple times to describe who He is, especially in John (6:35; 8:12; 10:9. 11'11:25; 14:6; 15:1). Jesus insisted that He spoke the truth He heard from God (Jn. 8:40) and knew Abraham, who had been dead for thousands of years. Jesus said, *"Before Abraham was born, I AM."* This infuriated the Jews, and they attempted to stone Him, because they knew the title I AM belonged only to the God who had met with Moses (Jn. 8:58-59). Seeing a man so young saying such things, they could not comprehend that He had lived that many years ago. To them, Jesus was a young man committing blasphemy.

The One who dealt directly with humans in both the Old and New Testaments was Jesus Christ, God the Son. In each incident, it was Jesus with whom men met and communicated. Further support is that Jesus said no man had seen His Father in any form, and we know God met with men in different appearances. Therefore, Jesus met with men as an angel, a man in human form, a smoking pot, a cloud, fire, and other forms. He took these images because God is spirit (Jn. 4:24), and no man could see the face of His spirit and live (Ex. 33:20, 23). Thus, Moses was only allowed to see Jesus' back.

In addition, New Testament writers confirm Jesus as being God who dealt with men in the Old Testament. Paul explained that when Moses led the people, they ate spiritual food and drank spiritual drink, from the spiritual rock that accompanied them. The rock was Christ who provided the Israelites water from the rock that Moses struck (1Cor. 10: 5). John explained the Son was seen in Isaiah's temple vision (1 Cor.12:41). Paul called Jesus the seed of Abraham (Gal.3:16-17).

Each place the phrase 'in the midst of' is used, it means God the Son is present. As God the Son, He was the man who wrestled with Jacob to ensure he treated Esau as he should. He spoke with Moses, and He was the fourth person in the midst of the fire as told by Daniel.

During Moses leadership, when the Israelites sinned, Jesus sent serpents to bite them, and Moses pleaded for their help. God had Moses make a bronze serpent and all who looked to it were healed. While on earth, Jesus referred to this example, telling people *"Like Moses lifted up the snake, the **Son of Man, who came from heaven** must be lifted up so that everyone who believes in Him may have eternal life."* (Jn. 3: 14-15 my emphasis).

Jesus told the people that if God was their Father, they would love Him because He came from God (Father) and was sent by the Father (Jn. 8:42). When accused of blasphemy, He said, *"I am God's Son"* (Jn. 10:36). After reading Isaiah 61 in the synagogue, Jesus told the men, *"Today this Scripture has been fulfilled in your hearing"* (Lk. 4:18-21).

Jesus said He had come down from heaven to do the will of Him who had sent Him (Jn. 6:38). Again, He told people He came from heaven, *"I am the living bread that came down from heaven"* (Jn. 6:51; 33, 35, 41, 58). Many not only failed to understand, but His words had many abandoning Him.

Jesus attempted to have people understand He was God, and was with God, and represented God, His Father. He wanted them to know He and the Father were bonded in perfectly unified deity. But few understood Jesus' meanings, no matter how many miracles He performed.

Recall that after Jesus' resurrection, He walked with two disciples. *"Beginning with Moses and all the Prophets, He explained to them what was said in **all** the Scriptures concerning*

Himself" (Lk. 24:27 my emphasis). Note: to tell them about Himself, He began with the Old Testament Scriptures. The theme of the Bible from Genesis through Revelation is Jesus Christ and how He works to redeem fallen humanity.

Jesus not only used Old Testament references to prove His identity, but many Old Testament authors foretold of Jesus being sent from the Father to do a task on earth. In the Old Testament, He is seen as an angel and at times, Jesus called to men from heaven (Ge. 16:7; 22:11-18; Jdg. 5:23; Isa. 55:10; Ps. 107:19-20, 147:15-18; 2 Ki. 19:35; Dan. 3:25). While angels did carry messages for Him (Heb. 2:2), we know angels do not call others My people or call themselves the God of your Fathers, as is written in Exodus (3: 2-6). It was Jesus. An angel did not tell Abraham that you did not withhold your son from Me (Ge. 22:11-12). Jesus told him. He identified Himself as the One calling to Paul from heaven, asking, "Why are you persecuting Me?" (Ac. 9:5). All such incidents were the Word, Jesus, speaking words the Father wanted said to mankind.

Likewise, many Old Testament writers foretold things that would occur in Jesus' life during New Testament times. For example, we find His virgin birth in Bethlehem (Isa. 7:14; Mic. 5:2; Lk. 1:35), His ministry of healing (Ge. 3:15; I Jn. 3:8), and His resurrection (Ps. 16:9-11; Ac. 2:31) are in both the Old and New Testaments. They foretold of Jesus' life, death, and resurrection, but few understood the prophets' meanings.

This means it was Jesus, the Word, Son of God, who acted according to man's needs by being both firm and stern and kind and gentle when each was appropriate for having mankind be faithful. Yes, Jesus sent unimaginable plagues on the Egyptian Pharaoh, punished Israelites by allowing their captivity by other nations, and destroyed many for idol worship. But His tenderness and gentleness are also recorded in the Old Testament. Read Psalm 86:5, Deuteronomy 10:18, Nahum 7:18-19, and Isaiah 40:11. Jeremiah 31 is especially telling of His love for people.

In New Testament times, Jesus Christ condemned idol worship, and He stressed the importance of worshipping only His Father. He repeated that one's love of God is to be man's most important relationship. He spoke more about the horrors of hell than other Bible teachers, and He was severely harsh when condemning sin and disrespect for His Father (Mt. 6:2, 21:12, 23:13, 18:17; Mk. 8:33; Lk. 11:42; Jn. 2: 13-7). No matter the time, date, or location, Jesus dealt with mankind as their words and actions required.

Throughout history, when God wanted to do work on earth that supported people being saved, He chose a specific man who would trust, believe, and obey God – simply because

21

the man believed that God was the true God, and his belief was strong enough to have him obey. The man represented the people he led and lived with. He acted as the people's leader who made a Covenant with the Lord. The intent was for them to have a relationship with the Lord, but more often they interpreted it as a performance-based agreement, and they failed often.

Covenants were binding agreements that told men what God required of them. Men could not make a Covenant with the Lord; only God could establish their Covenant. Men could make Covenants with other men or with themselves, as Job did with himself when he committed that he would not look lustfully at a girl (31:1). Most Covenants were enacted through some type of ritual or ceremony. All Covenants with God included blood because as the Bible says, the life of the flesh is in the blood (Lev. 17:11); for it is the life of all flesh (Lev. 7:14); …for the blood is the life (Dt. 12:23). Some Covenants included a celebration feast.

God's Covenants contained promises for mankind's obedience and a cruse with punishment for disobedience. Covenants confirmed that a selected man (and the people he led) had a bonded relationship with the Lord. The relationship is what makes them so important and why God kept accepting the people back after they broke their promise to obey. When people strayed from the Lord, they eventually became miserable and wanted to return to the Lord. He responded to their pleas because of His Covenant promise, not because of what men promised to do. God has always kept His Covenant promises and required that mankind live in dedicated devotion to their agreement to receive His promises.

Biblical Scriptures share men's' strengthens, weaknesses, doubts, and their worst sins so we can identify with them, as we too are sinners. This lets us realize how God's grace is given to all who regret their sins, change, and return to Him. The Holy Spirit hid nothing from us nor did He paint any person as being perfect as He directed men to write our Bible (2 Pe. 1:20-21; 2 Tim. 3:16-17).

Each Covenant included the man's descendant or seed. This inheritance did not depend on obedience to the Mosaic Law, but on God's grace of a Covenant promise to Abraham (Gal. 3: 8,9,14,28,29). By the use of specific men, the plan the Father, Son, and Spirit made in heaven would one day see complete fulfillment.

Knowing how each Covenant progressed helps to better understand the Godhead's plan for saving us. *Know therefore that the LORD your God is God; He is the faithful God, keeping His Covenant of love to a thousand generations of those who love Him and keep His commands* (Dt. 7:9).

Covenants contributed to God building an eternal family to live with Him in heaven. Each Covenant builds upon the prior one, until reaching the final New Covenant with Christ dying and His blood satisfying the price we owe the Father for our sins. Covenants are what tie together the many stores in the Bible. The last Covenant reveals Jesus Christ's relationship with us. It provides the promise of heaven through permanent forgiveness of our sins, and requires our commitment to obey, remain faithful, and help others.

Covenants explain the Scripture *'Salvation comes from the Lord'* (Jnh. 2:9). By Jesus Christ coming and solving the problem of our sin, He freed us from a fear of dying and left us with a firm hope of spending eternity as part of the Godhead's holy family. When we sin and repent, God promises permanent forgiveness, and He remembers our sin no longer. *Because Jesus lives forever, He is able to save completely those who come to God through Him, because **He always lives to intercede for them*** (Heb. 7:25; Ro. 8:34 my emphasis). With Jesus defending us to His Father, we can't lose.

Their plan was for Jesus Christ to take our sinfulness on Himself at the cross and give us His righteousness with our baptism, so we become good enough to live in heaven as His family. *Both the One who makes men holy and those who are made holy are of the **same family**. So, Jesus is not ashamed to call them* *brothers* (Heb. 2:11 my emphasis). And we, today, are included among those brothers.

In the remainder of this book, Jesus is the one being discussed where it uses Him, God, Lord, or the Word.

If the Father is intended, He is called Father.

JOIN THE MINORITY IN HEAVEN

A story is told of the meanest man in town being killed during a fight with the father of a young girl he had raped and set fire to the father's truck. Seems the dead man was feared by many and noted as the town's worst troublemaker.

The brother of the dead man threatened the small town's only preacher, telling him, "*I expect you to speak at my brother's funeral, and if you don't say only nice things about him, I will shoot you and your wife.*" The minister had no doubt that he meant it.

The minister called numerous people, asking them for something good the dead man had done for them or for the town. Not one person had a nice thing to say about the deceased. Most said the town was a better and safer place with the man gone.

The minister struggled for hours trying to decide what he could say. Then he had an idea. At the funeral, the minister stood, smiled, and thanked the brother and one guest for coming and said a brief prayer. Then he said, "*I could say a lot about this man, but I think the very best I can say about him is that he isn't the meanest man in this town. In fact, he isn't nearly as bad nor has he caused as much trouble as his brother."* The minister said another brief prayer for the man's family and the town's people to now find peace. Then he turned and raced out the back door.

The brother was never seen again. However, he posted a huge sign in front of his house that read: You don't know my brother's problems. He's in heaven now, so stop talking bad about him.

Have you ever heard anyone say their loved one is in hell, no matter his spiritual condition? We all want to believe those we love and think were good people will go to heaven, even if we may know it's likely a false belief.

What's so heartbreaking is that Jesus tells us that many more will go to hell than heaven. It's especially sad because God wants everyone to be saved. In 2 Peter (3:9 my emphasis) we read that God wants all to repent so none perish. *"The Lord is not slow in keeping His promise, as some understand slowness. He is patient with you,* **not wanting anyone to perish, but everyone come to repentance.**"

Jesus promises us heaven, but He requires our commitment to obey and remain faithful: **Make every effort** to enter through the narrow door, because many, I tell you, will try to enter, and will not be able (Lk. 13:24, my emphasis).

That's because *in his pride the wicked does not seek Him, in all his thoughts there is no room for God* (Ps. 10:4).

Jesus explained that many who try to enter the narrow door will hear, *"I don't know you or where you come from. Away from me, all you evildoers! There will be weeping there, and gnashing of teeth, when you see Abraham, Isaac, and Jacob, and all the prophets in the kingdom of God, but you yourselves thrown out"* (Lk. 13:24-28). Remaining faithful to Jesus is essential for living in heaven because the curse's punishment for disobedience is eternity in hell. The cowardly, unbelieving, vile, murderers, sexually immoral, those who practice magic arts, idolaters, and all liars will be in the fiery lake of burning sulfur, the second death (Rev. 21:8), but he who overcomes will be My son, and I will be his God (v. 7).

Because this message is so important, Jesus provided another similar caution in Matthew (7:13-14*): Enter through the narrow gate. For wide is the gate and broad is the road that leads to destruction, and many enter through it. But small is the gate and narrow the road that leads to life, and only a few find it.* Jesus calls Himself the gate through whom His sheep would come to be saved (Jn. 10:7-9).

In the very next verses (Jn.10:15-16), Jesus explained why so many will be condemned to hell: many listen to false teachers who bear bad fruit. These teachers and those who follow them will hear, *"I never knew you. Away from me you evil-doers"* (v.23). He was telling them that they had broken the Covenant, and He planned to enforce the Covenant curse's punishment. The world is filled with many false teachers today who call themselves men of the cloth, preachers, ministers, priests, and sadly, all have followers. They teach what they want God's Word to say, not what it actually says. God has never allowed men to edit or change what He teaches: *Do not add to what I command you, and do not subtract from it* (Dt. 4:2). Even Jesus followed completely all that His Father commanded Him to say and do (Jn. 12:49-50; 14:31). God's way is narrow, but what a promise we have for walking it.

Jesus said, "I am the Way, the Truth, and the Life and no one comes to the Father but through Me (Jn. 14:6). We have no Lord but Jesus. There is one faith and that faith was given by Jesus Christ. Jesus promised the apostles that He would lead them into all truth (Jn. 16:13). We are to contend for the truth that was once for all time delivered to the saints (Jude 3). We are told to adhere strictly to the Scriptures as provided, not change any, for their truth leads to eternal salvation. We must not turn from it to other teachings of men because they can only lead us to living a sinful life. It's why personal study of His word is so important for ensuring what is being taught is accurate. We have no Lord but Jesus, and the Bible is our source of measurement for what is truth. Faith and obedience to Jesus Christ distinguishes those on the narrow path from those taking the road to destruction.

Our life on earth is a training ground to prepare believers for living in heaven, and knowing God's word ensures we know right and truth from wrong and lies. There are many lessons we need to learn while living here. For example, we need to learn to listen when called by the Lord to be baptized and when called to help others. It's an inner knowing, an inner feeling, an instruction given by Jesus' Holy Spirit letting us know that today I need to make lunch for an ill friend, or need to spend more time with my toddler, or go apologize to someone. It's when we admit there is a sin in our life that we must entirely abandon, or how I must react as I face a fiery test that Jesus is presenting me. Jesus created us in His image to be like Him, and we must learn to listen and respond as we are shown ways we need to grow spiritually.

Life on earth is a training ground to prepare believers for living in heaven

All growth today is to strengthen us in goodness and dependence on the Lord. Our life on earth is a time to learn what it really means to belong to Jesus as His created being. It's learning to allow Him to be our God and our King and letting Him make our decisions as we strive to reduce our self-centeredness and self-control. It is learning to be comfortable with being the created, and Jesus the Creator. Us the subject, Him the Lord and King. If we aren't comfortable with Him as our King today, we aren't ready for heaven where He rules. It requires remembering **we were made by Him and for Him** (Col. 1:16 my emphasis). Jesus is Lord of this world and of heaven. We control neither. He is the power that holds everything together (Col. 1:17). Think about what that means and where we would be if He decided He is tired of how we behave. Yet, He keeps loving us. We must believe that since Jesus loved us enough to die in our place, He loves us enough to take care of our every need and us let go and let Him.

Yet, how many people do you think take every decision to God before acting? If every person, who never seeks His guidance or asks for His help except during a serious crisis, immediately disappeared, how many people would be left where you live? Would you be among the breathing?

We may refuse to honor Jesus today as our Creator, God, King, Lord, and Savior, but God the Father promises we will one day show Jesus the respect He's due: *God exalted Him to the highest place and gave Him the name that is above every name, that at the name of Jesus every knee should bow, in heaven and on earth and under the earth, and every tongue confess that Jesus Christ is Lord to the glory of the Father* (Phil. 2:9-11). If that is our first time to honor Him, it will also be our last because heaven will belong to others.

Our time on earth is a training ground for living in heaven because if we won't allow Him to be our Lord here, He won't be our Savior when we leave here. Remember there can be no sin in heaven, so heaven must reject rebels. As you study the Scriptures, note that every place Lord and Savior are mentioned together, He's always listed as Lord before Savior and for a reason that we should take seriously.

Man is unique. No other created being is made in God's image, nor is said to have a soul. Mankind was the only creation made to have relationship with the Lord. We were made for intimacy with Him. Remember, Jesus even keeps count of every hair on our heads (Mt. 10:30). Think about how close that requires Him to stay to each of us. Every time we wash or brush our hair, Jesus has to do another recount. Before a thought is formed, He knows what we are thinking (Ps. 139:4). He knows the motives driving our thoughts (1 Chron. 28:9), and the thoughts controlling our actions. Jesus sends His Holy Spirit to stay constantly with us because He wants to help us live a life that guarantees eternity with Him. Remember, with our baptism, He sends His Holy Spirit who lives in our inner being, in our hearts (Ro. 5:5; Jn. 14:16-17; Eph. 3:16-17).

However, following Jesus, ensures we will face spiritual battles, but it also ensures He will be with us, giving us the strength needed to remain faithful. We're told to cast our cares on the Lord, and He will sustain us; He will never let the righteous fall (Ps. 55:22). Yet, the plea of Jesus still rings as true today as when He said, *"How often I have longed to gather your children together, as a hen gathers her chicks under her wings, but you were not willing"* (Lk. 13:34). The lesson is to learn to trust that the Lord cares about every detail of our lives, and give control to Him. He pleads to take care of us and provide for all our needs. But it requires our making Him the most important One in our lives, and He tells us, *"If you love me, you will obey what I command"* (Jn. 14:15). If we are going to wear Christ's name (Christ-ian) our behaviors and words must show we trust Him and strive to live as He asks.

He is to be the One we turn to before seeking advice or comfort from another, because others are nothing more than another earthly being that He also created. We must learn to put the Creator before the created, because no matter our issues, all our battles are spiritual. **We struggle not against flesh and blood, but with Satan** and his dark, spiritual forces of evil (Eph. 6:12 my emphasis). When caught in a

34

heartbreaking situation, we tend to blame another person, without realizing it is Satan who must be defeated, and only Jesus helps us do that.

When caught in a heartbreaking situation, we tend to blame another person, without realizing it is Satan who must be defeated, and only Jesus helps us do that

Night and day Satan labors to thwart God's plan for saving us. The evil in this world is the work of the powers of darkness, and Satan is the leader in charge. He never relaxes or takes a break in his opposition to God's plan of redeeming us. Satan uses people and even objects and events that might cause us to sin. Satan doesn't just want us disobeying God's laws and committing multiple sins; he wants us doubting God and judging Him as wrong to ask of us what He does. Satan wants us thinking we can make better judgments, which is nothing but an attempt to replace God with ourselves as god. How Satan must smile when we do that. Remember that's the same type thinking that got Adam and Eve in trouble. Satan always has us ignoring the many ways God blesses us just as He did Adam and Eve who originally enjoyed a perfect lifestyle.

Thankfully, Jesus didn't leave us hanging, questioning if anyone could be saved with Satan working so hard to devour us (1 Pe.5:8). Scriptures assure us that, because Jesus suffered when He was tempted, He is able to help us when we are tempted (Heb. 2:18). God keeps a tight rein on Satan and will not let him hurt us beyond what we can handle. *God is faithful; He will not let you be tempted beyond what you can bear. But when you are tempted, He will also provide a way out so you can stand up under it* (1 Cor. 10:13). It's one reason we are commanded to pray without ceasing. We need God's help to remain faithful, but we must ask for His help. As with God's Covenant promises, He requires obligations for men to fulfill. And when He asks something of us, He always tells us how to satisfy His command.

As Jesus walked on earth, there were many people who followed Him because He fed them, but He told these people they were to work for food that endures to eternal life (Jn. 6:26). He explained that the work of God is to believe in the One whom God had sent (v.33). Jesus promised, *"My Father's will is that everyone who looks to the Son and believes in Him shall have eternal life, and I will raise him up at the last day"* (v.40). We are required to believe that Jesus died in our place, was resurrected, and with faithful obedience, we too will be resurrected from the dead to live forever with Him in heaven.

In his interesting book, Foundations of Grace, Stephen Lawson, compares the story of creation to our salvation: God's dazzling display of sovereignty in creation was a primer on His right to rule in matters of salvation. God, who commanded the light to appear on day one of creation, soon would order gospel light to shine into the darkened hearts of spiritually blind sinners. God, who separated the waters on day two, would cause an infinite chasm to separate Himself from sinners. God, who gathered the waters together on day three, would gather sinners to Himself. God, who created the sun, moon, and stars on day four, would omnipotently create saving faith. God, who began to create the animal kingdom on day five, would graciously send His Son to be the Lamb of God to take away sin. God, who created Adam and Eve on day six, would re-create sinners into His image. His free grace would perform the second Genesis in the salvation of lost men and women.

Jesus assured us that people of all races and nations who keep His Covenant go to heaven. People will come from east and west and north and south, and will take their places at the feast in the kingdom of God (Lk. 13:29).

In addition, we know when the apostle John looked into heaven, he saw such a huge multitude of people wearing white robes that no one could count them. John was told that those wearing white robes had washed their robes and made them white in the blood of the Lamb (Jesus Christ). Washing their robes in the blood of Jesus was the act of being cleansed of sin through their faith in Him and being buried by baptism (Rev. 22:14; 7:13-14).

John then described what the saved were doing in heaven: *They are before the throne of God and serve Him day and night in His temple; and He who sits on the throne will spread His tent over them. Never again will they hunger; never again will they thirst. The sun will not beat upon them, nor any scorching heat. For the Lamb at the center of the throne will be their shepherd; He will lead them to springs of living water. And God will wipe away every tear from their eyes* (Rev. 7:17).

Heaven requires that we are washed in the blood of Christ by being buried in baptism (Ro. 6:4), and then applying Jesus' commands in how we behave and think (Col. 3:17). Yet, we know that we all sin and fall short (Ro. 3:23). It's because we know how badly we fail that we fear Jesus' second coming. We are terrified about meeting God, and yet, at the same time, we cherish the thought of living forever in Paradise where there's never sin or discomfort, thanking Jesus for paying the price we owed for our sins, and seeing again our departed loved ones. God has placed within us a desire for immortality; He set eternity in the hearts of men (Ecc. 3:11).

SATAN DOESN'T CHANGE

Some of the following chapters provide mini-reviews of Covenants God made with specific men. They prove how faithful God remained to His promises, even as men continually disobeyed. We can learn useful lessons from the stories about each person. An attempt is made to note what each man did that had God honoring them with blessings, what they did that disappointed or angered the Lord, and how often we are like each man. See if you can identify with and learn from them. We aren't to just know God's word but we are to learn to do it.

For example, remember how Adam and Eve weren't long in the perfect garden before they sinned? By Genesis chapter 3, Satan was planting doubt in Eve's mind about the Lord's commands. Satan convinced her that she could be wise like the Lord (lust of pride), thinking the fruit looked appealing (lust of the eyes), and appearing that it would taste good and satisfy her craving (lust of flesh). Eve caved to Satan's words and sinned. Years later, Satan used the same temptations when he tempted Jesus and uses the same ways to tempt you and me. John called the sins designed by Satan as **cravings** of sinful man, **lust** of his eyes, and **boasting** of what he has and does. John says these come from the world, not the Father (1 Jn. 2:16 my emphasis). Which type describes the last sin you committed? Craving? Lust? Boasting?

While the word Covenant was not used in Genesis as God dealt with Adam, Hosea (6:7) says Adam broke the Covenant. Like all of God's Covenants, Adam was given promises for obedience and punishment for disobedience. God gave him four commands: be fruitful and multiply (Ge. 1:28), rule over the fish, birds, and every living creature that moved on the earth (1: 28), eat only seed-bearing plants (v.29), and work and care for the garden (2:15). Adam was granted the privilege of naming Eve and every animal (2:19, 23; 3:30). He shared perfect fellowship with the Lord. *They heard the sound of the LORD God as He was walking in the garden in the cool of the day* (Ge. 3:8). Adam had only one negative command: You must not eat from the tree of the knowledge of good and evil. God forewarned Him of the punishment for disobeying: *when you eat of it, you will surely die* (Ge. 2:17). Adam knew in advance what God expected, and he was to tell Eve, because God gave Adam the Covenant before creating Eve (Ge. 15-18).

Satan chose the forbidden tree for tempting Eve, because he knew their forbiddance of touching this particular tree was God's source of power for keeping His human family protected from evil. But Eve listened to Satan and disobeyed

God. Then Adam proved he valued pleasing Eve more than he loved God. Instead, of acting as God's spokesperson and persuading Eve to stop, he submitted to her idea and also ate the forbidden fruit.

Adam and Eve could have eaten from the Tree of Life and forever known Jesus' righteousness. Instead, they chose Satan's sinful way over Jesus' saving way, something the majority of people do today.

Their decision showed rejection of God's right to rule and a declaration of themselves as independent of Him. They had decided to make their own rules. Then instead, of seeking the Lord's grace and forgiveness, Satan had them trying to hide from the Lord. They could have repented and known peace, but instead, they tried to conceal their nakedness - their exposed sin and shame - by making clothing for themselves from fig leaves.

Their decision to disobey was rejection of God's right to rule and a declaration of themselves as independent of Him

Satan was not finished Satan is never satisfied with just one sin; he goes after the whole person. Adam and Eve avoided responsibility for their choices, and their heightened self-consciousness had them focused on self-protection and care of self. They hoped to hide their sins, but God always knows every sin man commits. They were now a slave to Satan and feared God. They attempted to avoid God, which made matters worse. Satan had them turning against each other, blaming each other for their decisions. Adam blamed God and Eve, *"The woman **you put here** with me – she gave me some fruit from the tree, and I ate it."* Eve blamed the serpent. How we do the same. When upset, we immediately think – not what did I do wrong – but how the other person wronged me or hurt me. Then Satan wins again.

Satan is never satisfied with just one sin; he goes after the whole person.

Romans (6:16 my emphasis) explains: *Don't you know that when you offer yourselves to someone to obey him as slaves, **you are slaves to the one whom you obey** – whether you are slaves to sin, which leads to death, or to obedience which leads to righteousness?* Adam and Eve had chosen to obey Satan, so when they heard God coming, they attempted to hide among the trees (Ge. 3:7-10). But like God does for His disobedient children who attempt to hide, He pursued them. When God asked, "Where are you?" it showed how lost Adam and Eve lived. Still, God's enquiry showed He didn't want to leave them this way. They knew they had broken fellowship with Him, and they were about to learn that a man-made solution for hiding sin never works. Had they admitted their sin, and pleaded for the

Lord's forgiveness, they could have restored their relationship with the Lord. But they didn't.

God's immediate punishment was to ensure they could never eat of the Tree of Life and live forever in their sinful condition. To ensure they obeyed this time, God banned them from the Garden. They learned that sin always carries negative consequences.

Although He punished Adam and Eve for their sinful decisions, the Lord continued caring for them. No matter how far or how fast people run from the Lord, God pursues them to bring them home. Adam and Eve needed awakening from their selfish slavery to sin and realize the depth of their wrong. Jesus would not let His first children remain lost.

Even today, He actively purses believers who keep trying to run away. God tests them with hope they remember Him, turn back, and realize He can give them peace and forgiveness. God longs to bring all sinners home to live under His care today and with Him in heaven throughout eternity.

Previously, Adam and Eve had been allowed to eat only vegetables, fruit, and seeds (1:18), so the animals would have time to reproduce and fill the earth with their own kind (1:24). But to cover their sin, Jesus sacrificed an animal to make them garments of skin to wear. (3:21). This animal was the first recorded sacrifice of blood used to cover man's sin. God's grace symbolized what would come years later as numerous sacrifices of animal blood, and Jesus' blood would follow.

Their new clothing was a gift from God, and the animal was a true victim who shed his blood for them. Since Adam's day in the Garden, instead of a guilty man paying the blood price that's due for his sins, God has always required another to pay the penalty in the sinner's place. What love God has continued to show and what forgiveness He grants when we run to Him, crying, *"Holy Father, I have sinned. Please forgive me for. . . Restore my relationship with you, and protect me from Satan."*

After Adam's and Eve's disobedience, their life changed dramatically in spiritual, emotional, and physical ways they could never have foreseen. They were now well aware of losing their secure relationship with the Lord and knew how it felt to fear Him. They could no longer walk and talk with Jesus in the Garden. This spiritual fellowship was dead. Emotionally, they were no longer loving but becoming self-centered and blaming each other for their bad decisions. In addition, they soon grasped the full meaning of physical death and dying and learned it in ways no parent wants to know. They had to face the death of their younger son, Abel, when he was killed by Cain, their firstborn. They learned about death, human anger, and the consequences of sin beyond anything they could have imagined before sinning.

Abel had brought the fat portion from the first-born of his flock as an offering to the Lord, and Cain brought 'some' food he had raised. Obviously, Cain's 'some' was such a small amount that it wasn't a genuine sacrifice, while Abel gave up a first-born animal. God has always demanded our very best. It appears Cain did not have a heart that wanted to honor the Lord and attempted to serve Him half-heartedly.

Malachi (3:6-18) cautions us not to rob God of titles and offerings. Look at the activities you do because you love the Lord and the money you give. Is it a token giving of 'some?' Are you sacrificing, or are you robbing God?

God gave Cain a second chance to receive forgiveness, by saying if he would do what's right and master sin, he would be accepted. Instead of doing a soul-searching evaluation and repenting, Cain asked his brother to go to a field, where in angry jealousy Cain murdered Abel. John (1 Jn.3:12) tells us he murdered his brother because his actions were evil, and his brothers were righteous. Still, God gave Cain a third opportunity to change by asking where his brother was. Instead of admitting his wrong, Cain lied, pretending he didn't know.

Seven things are an abomination to the Lord (Prov. 6:16-19). God hates these sins: haughty eyes because pride and arrogance keep one from repenting, lying, shedding innocent blood, a heart that devises wicked plans, feet that run to be involved in doing evil, false witnesses who lie, and one who stirs up trouble and discord among brothers. Cain was guilty.

God punished Cain by sending him away from his family, as a wanderer working ground that would no longer yield good crops. God said Abel's blood had cried out to Him, and He sent Cain away from His presence. Cain pleaded, *"Whoever finds me will kill me."* God marked him to ensure this did not happen.

Cain's fearing others, showed Adam and Eve had other children by then, and we're told Cain left with a wife, obviously a sister or cousin, who supported him. They built a city out of the Lord's presence, and began the worship of idols. Mankind divided by those who loved and served the Lord versus those who chose to abandon God's authority.

What horrible differences Adam and Eve encountered as a result of disobeying the Lord. It shows how sin passes from generation to generation when children observe parents living willful, sinful lives, and they are not taught about the Lord.

Still, my heart aches reading about Adam and Eve. Losing one's child would be agonizing, but knowing he was killed by his brother would be unbearable. I understand some of their pain. Three years ago, I received a call saying my older son, Todd, had a swimming accident and was totally paralyzed. I live 1500 miles away and could not get a flight for two days. When I arrived, he appeared worse than my imagination had envisioned. Doctors had cut open his neck in the front and back to attach wires to his spine. He was in good spirits, but hallucinating badly, seeing tiny pink helicopters flying about and thinking the nurses were going to kill me. My second day, he began telling me he couldn't breathe. I assumed he was confused, until a couple of hours later, when he began gasping and chocking. I stepped to the hall. No nurse or doctor was in sight. I stood screaming for help! Within minutes, the entire crisis team arrived. They punctured his neck where a baseball sized blood clot had formed. Blood splatter the wall, floor, and bed. They asked my permission to rush him back to surgery and cut his neck open again, saying if I had not been there, he would have died. Still, without this second surgery he would die and with it. . . How helpless one feels when it is your child whom doctors say might die. I prayed. I cried. I had never known such stress. I understand some of the emotions Adam and Eve experienced hearing their son had died. How could parents handle such heartache? Unlike how Cain acted, Todd's brother came and stayed two weeks helping organize Todd's finances. He even cut Todd's toe nails before leaving.

And I am still in the doghouse with his sister for asking her to wait until he left rehab to come, for fear, he would need help longer than I could stay. I cannot imagine the pain I would have experienced if one of them had murdered Todd. Today, Todd walks with a shuffle, his fingers don't work well, and he's in constant pain. But he is alive. Weekly, after moving Todd to rehab, they talked with me about him possibly spending the rest of his life in a nursing home, and my stress seemed unbearable. But unlike Eve, I didn't have to bury a son and mourn his brother killing him. Surely, the loss of two sons contributed to Adam and Eve changing and rearing a grandson who worshipped the Lord. But what unbelievably agonizing pain they had to experience.

Also significant is the clothing God gave Adam and Eve. Throughout Scripture clothing is used to describe both sin and righteousness. Isaiah (64:6) describes sin as filthy rags: *All of us have become like one who is unclean, and all our righteous acts are like filthy rags; we all shrivel up like a leaf.* Certainly, Adam and Eve were unprepared for coping with a shriveling of their fig leaves. They required something better. Interestingly, Psalm (1:3) says the way to keep a leaf from withering is to meditate on the Lord day and night. Obviously, Adam and Eve failed to keep the Lord in their thoughts. This Scripture is a reminder that we cannot be righteous on our own, nor save ourselves, and even our best-efforts pale in comparison to what we are capable of doing if we depend on the Lord.

Isaiah says *He has clothed me with garments of salvation and a robe of righteousness* (61:10). That is surely why God gave Adam and Eve new clothing. He wanted to forgive their sin, inflict their punishment for deliberate disobedience, and make them acceptable again. They also needed to realize their sin caused the death of an innocent animal.

A similar example is found in Zechariah (3:4) that gives the angel's message to Joshua to remove sin and walk in the Lord's ways. *Take off his filthy clothes. Then He said to Joshua, "See I have taken away your sin, and I will put rich garments on you." They put a clean turban on his head and clothed him, while the angel of the Lord stood by.* The change of clothing was the removing of sin, and with obedience, came forgiveness and a promise of God's care. It was what Jesus did for Adam and Eve, and yearns to do for us.

Still, God had to punish Adam and Eve. Man may be forgiven, but he still suffers the consequences of his sin. Jesus would not be a just God to set a rule and then ignore its disobedience. If He did, people could not fully trust what He told them and would always wonder if He really meant it this time. . . or not.

Because the serpent allowed Satan to use him, God punished him by making him crawl on his belly in dirt all of his life. He became one of the most hated of all animals. God told Satan He was going to crush his head by Jesus being resurrected after Satan stroke Jesus' heel. God would offer mankind grace by promising triumph over Satan through the offspring of woman (Ge. 3:15). Years later, Mary's son, Jesus, would die on the cross and be resurrected to reign at the right hand of God, with Satan condemned to hell.

Eve's punishment left her desiring her man's love, while Adam would rule the amount and type of loving time and attention he gave her. She was to forever submit to his rule -- as he submitted to God's. In addition, Eve would now experience pain in childbirth (v.16), as God blessed them with more children.

Because Adam listened to his wife (v. 17), instead of continuing to just enjoy the privilege of ruling over the fish, birds, livestock, and other creatures (1:26), he also had to painfully toil by the sweat of his brow as he worked to care for his family.

Because of Adam's sin, the earth was cursed. It would now produce thorns and thistles, as man attempted to raise plants of the field. (3:17-19).

The sins of Adam and Eve introduced death, disease, pain, and suffering into the world. From the results of their sin, to some degree, we are all punished. All people have to choose between good and evil and are tempted to base their decision on what's most beneficial for self: what I want, and what I like. *Sin entered the world through one man, and death through sin, and in this way, death came to all men* (Ro. 5:12).

While a piece of fruit may seem insignificant, Jesus demonstrated how serious He is about His commands being obeyed. He showed how His commands are designed for mankind's protection and how disobedience has immediate and long-term consequences.

Hebrews (12:11) explains that *No discipline seems pleasant at the time, but painful. Later on, however, it produces a harvest of righteousness and peace for those who have been trained by it*. It appears that after an animal's blood had been sacrificed for Adam and Eve to cover their shame of sin, they followed the Lord. We know they had another son, Seth. After Seth had a son, called Enosh, Scripture says, "M*en began to call on the name of the Lord*" (4:26). We hope that was because Adam acted like God's family leader and taught his children about the Lord.

What a stern message Adam's punishment is for men who let their wives influence them to do wrong and for women who refuse to submit to what the husband knows is right with the Lord. Adam was designed to be the leader-teacher of his family, teaching Eve and their children about the Lord. The Lord had told Adam what to eat and touch and what not to (2:16). It was his role to lead in ensuring they were obedient, and Eve's role was to follow all leadership that obeys the Lord. A similar message of women being submissive to their husbands is continued in the New Testament, with men expected to ensure their family's obedience to the Lord, and women's' role to act in ways that support their compliance to God's commands (Eph. 5:22).

Although the gate to heaven is narrow, even when mankind failed and disrespected the Lord, He always provided a way for them to be forgiven. Cain had three chances to change. That's how deeply God wants us with Him throughout eternity. He remains eager to forgive our sinful ways and ensues we know what His forgiveness requires.

Adam lived many more years and had more sons and daughters. Their children married siblings, cousins, or nieces/nephews. We know because Acts 17:26 explains that *from one man He made every nation of men, and Adam named his wife Eve because she would become the mother of all living (Ge. 3:20).* Incest was not wrong until the earth was well populated, and God gave the Law through Moses. Until then, the gene pool was obviously healthy enough that it caused no problems. More importantly, those who followed the Lord did not want their children marrying Canaanites (Cain's ancestry) who worshipped idols, for that would ensure an ungodly influence throughout their blood line.

Christ came to offer us a way to be forgiven of our disobedience and to have a better promise. In Romans (5:19) we find: *For just as through the disobedience of the one man (Adam) the many were made sinners, so also through the obedience of the one man (Christ) the many will be made righteous.* Paul reminded the Corinthians that *God (Father)made Him (Christ) who had no sin to be sin for us, so that* **in Him we** *might* **become the righteousness of God** (2 Cor. 5:21 my emphasis).

Peter explained, *He Himself bore our sins in His body on the tree, so that we might die to sins and live for righteousness; by His wounds you have been healed. For you were like sheep going astray, but now you have returned to the Shepherd and Overseer of your souls* (1 Pe. 2:24-25).

No matter what sins a person commits, God never leaves that person without a way to be forgiven and retain hope of heaven. He gave Cain three opportunities. Why? Because no matter how man disobeys, God always keeps His Covenant promises.

WHO GOD WANTS YOU TO MARRY

When my husband and I toured the Holy Land and rode from Jerusalem to the Sea of Galilee, we saw numerous small villages with 10-15 large, tall houses per group. Our tour guide said the only way one could live in that clan's village was to be born there or marry into it. He explained. *When the first-born son marries, if his parents are alive, he builds another floor atop the house to live with his bride."* Thus, some houses were four or five stories tall because the parent's firstborn son and this son's first-born son and each first-born son thereafter lived in the same house. The guide said, *"When the parents die, each couple and their children move downstairs one story, leaving the top floor open for the next first offspring son who weds."* While each couple lived in the same house with his parents, they lived as if they were miles away from each other in decision making, money control, and daily contact. They shared time together, during special events and worship.

A similar practice continues in Taiwan today. Each time my husband's Taiwanese coworker, Albert, visited the United States, we invited him for dinner. Albert shared that he and his wife were currently dating their son's girlfriend. Albert explained that once his son became interested enough in a woman to consider asking her to marry him, the son's family started going with them as they dated. This was to ensure his family liked her, and she liked them. He explained this was important because when a son married, the new wife would move into the house with him and his parents. I asked, *"What would happen if the young man's mother and girlfriend did not like each other?"* Albert replied, *"Then he will not marry this girl, but find another, because she must live with us and have peace."* It seems as Old Testament people moved about, the idea of living within the man's clan spread to many places.

As God blessed men with large herds of cattle, they moved about to have enough pasture, and the number of evil men increased at a greater pace than men who continued to follow the Lord. Cain had moved to the land of Nod, away from the Lord's presence (Ge. 4:16). He built a city, and his sons and many great, great grandsons migrated and populated the earth without knowing the Lord and became increasing wicked.

Adam's family through his son, Seth, had reared nine generations when Noah was born, making Noah the tenth from Adam. Adam had Seth when he was 130 years old. Altogether Adam lived 930 years, and he was still alive when Noah's father was born. When Seth was 105 years old, he had Enosh, lived another 807 years, and had other children.

During these years, men called on the name of the Lord (Ge. 4:26).

Seth's son, Enosh, was 90 when he had Kenan, and he lived another 815 years and had other sons and daughters. Kenan had Mahalalel when he was70, and he lived 840 more years and had other sons and daughters. When Mahalalel was 65, he became the father of Jared, lived another 830 years and had more sons and daughters. Jared became the father of Enoch when he was 162, lived another 800 years and had other sons and daughters. At age 65, Enoch had Methuselah and he walked with God 300 years, as he had more sons and daughters. Enoch did not die for God took him away. So, we know some men worshipped the Lord through this generation.

Methuselah became the father of Lamech at age 187 and lived another 782 years, having more sons and daughters. Lamech was 182 when he had Noah, then he lived another 595 years, and had more children. By this time, the majority of men practiced idol worship.

Noah was 500 years old when he began having children (5:32), and men had become progressively more and more evil. Still, God called Noah a righteous man. By the time Noah's three sons married, they were the only eight people alive in the entire world who worshipped the Lord. God's promise of our redemption through the offspring of woman seemed like a lost concept.

Evilness spread as grandchildren of Cain and Seth disobeyed the Lord by intermarrying (Ge. 6:2). As their numbers greatly increased, they spread out and formed other clans or groups. Often, the clan/group assumed the name of a male leader. By Genesis 6, most people had forgotten the Lord. In God's disappointment, He limited mankind's days on earth to 120 years (Ge. 6:3).

God continually reminded people of His promises to care for them, and still, they wanted to trust their own ideas instead of listening to Him. Such behavior reminds me of a parent who sees their young child attempting to put a paperclip into an electrical socket, and knowing how hurt the child will be if she succeeds. The parent realizes the child isn't going to stop no matter how strongly the parents call to the child. Only by taking away the child's free will, can the parent stop the child, which will teach the child nothing about the danger that's involved. And so, despite God's continued calls to obey and heed His warning, the Israelites continued to intermarry with idol worshippers and stray from Him.

Still, God reminded them of the dangers of idol worship: *Make no Covenant with them and show no mercy. Do not intermarry with them. Do not give your daughters to their sons for they will turn your sons away from following me to serve other gods, and the LORD'S anger will burn against you and will quickly destroy you.* **(Note it is daughters who more often turn men from the Lord)**. *This is what you are to do to them: Break down their altars, smash their sacred stones, cut down the Asherah poles and burn their idols in the fire. For you are a people holy to the LORD your God. The LORD your God has chosen you out of all the peoples on the face of the earth to be His people, His treasured possession (Dt. 7:2-6).* Loving them so strongly that He called them His treasured possession fell on deaf ears.

From that time in history through today, God has continued to forewarn of the dangers of believers marrying unbelievers. It has always been God's intent for a believer to marry another faithful believer. He repeatedly cautioned how adapting to another's unbelief or false teaching can cost one heaven.

It has always been God's intent for a believer to marry another faithful believer

Too often, people marry because of their feelings for another. They ignore God's command not to marry one who doesn't worship Him. Being made in God's image, we could learn to love a believer just as easily, and hopefully, easier because of sharing more core values. But people have continued to rebel and do things their way, not God's. This has caused them continued pain and hardships, as well as, costing many heaven. Few people today can say no one in their family has experienced divorce.

However, it should be noted that God's people were free to marry non-Israelites, provided the nonbeliever converted to worship God. For example, Ruth was a Moabite, Rahab a Canaanite, and Bathsheba's husband who served in King David's army was a Hittite. Still, far more believers turned away to follow their spouse's way of worship than the number of idol worshippers who learned to worship the Lord.

Among King David's wise words of advice for his son, he said: *"Above all else, guard your heart, for it is the wellspring of life"* (Prov. 4:23). How right David was. Who we marry, what we listen to, who we befriend, and things we share with others, all influence our decisions and shape both our daily existence and our eternal destiny. With godly marriages we have support for remaining faithful and raising godly children who will do the same so we enjoy eternity in heaven together.

From Genesis through Revelation, we read how God dealt harshly with unscriptural forms of worship. Yet, how often we fail to teach this to our children before they prepare for marriage. Then we wonder why we have so many divorces, generations of children who know not God, and who will find the narrow door to heaven bolted shut to them.

The same idea is carried in the New Testament. Paul cautioned Christians not to be unequally yoked with unbelievers (2 Cor. 6:14). Christians are the temple of God, and Paul asks, *"How can a temple of God share in worshipping idols?"* An idol is not always something made of gold or silver. It can be television, money, recreation, a career, or another person. An idol is anything/anyone that replaces the Lord and has people devoting more of their love, attention, money, and time, than to God. Recall how Adam loved Eve more than the Lord. We are to love God above all else. Many Christians have been spiritually, emotionally, and physically injured by being in unhappy marriages with worldly and unbelieving spouses. Too often, such Christians are lured to become unfaithful themselves and lose their souls.

By Noah's day, people had become violent and practiced idol worship, and the Lord regretted having made man. He decided to wipe mankind, and all animals, including the creatures that moved on the ground and birds of the air, from the face of the earth. Only Noah found favor in the eyes of the Lord (Ge. 6:8) because he was righteous and walked with God. (Ge. 6:9). Other Bible versions say Noah found grace from the Lord. Perhaps, he was influenced by his faithful great grandfather Enoch (Ge. 5:22). Even today, grandfathers who serve as spiritual leaders for their families leave heavenly legacies for their grandchildren.

God gave Noah the design for building a huge ark. Noah believed God and obeyed, *according to all that God commanded him, so he did* (Ge. 6:22). While working on this monumental task, Noah attempted to warn men of their coming doom. Peter described Noah as a preacher of righteousness (2 Pe. 2:5).

When the ark was completed, God had pairs of all unclean animals and seven of every kind of clean animal, male and female, come to Noah. Once the animals, Noah, his sons, Japheth, Shem, and Ham, and their wives were inside, God shut the door. (Ge. 7:16). God flooded the earth for 150 days (v. 24). Everything and everyone left on earth perished (v. 21).

How easily we forget how deeply God hates sin, and He will not tolerate disobedience forever. God is always in control of man's ultimate outcome, just as He was during Noah's day. Likewise, we should remember that the Lord always protects those who strive to follow Him, no matter how few there may be.

MORE PROOF GOD LOVES YOU

Have you ever wondered why you live where you do? Or asked, "Why do I live where I do, and not Iran, or Brazil, or Japan?" Or wondered, "Why am I living today and not 100 years ago or 50 years from now?"

God answers these questions in Acts (17:26-28 my emphasis): *From one man, He made every nation of men, that they should inhabit the whole earth; and He determined the times set for them and the exact places where they should live. God did this so that men would seek Him and perhaps reach out for Him and find Him, though He is not far from each one of us. For in Him, we live and move and have our being. We are His offspring.*

Note we are all the offspring of one man, Adam. Adam named his wife Eve because she would become the mother of all the living (Ge. 3;20). As God created our inmost being, He put special talents and abilities in each person that is to be used to help others (Eph. 2:10). God knit us in our mother's womb (Ps. 139:13), or we say in the South, He put the right sperm with the right egg and made it grow, and watched our unformed body develop (v. 15b). Before creation of the world, He chose us to be holy and blameless in His sight, and to be adopted as His sons and daughters, through Jesus Christ

(Eph. 1:5). He was personally involved in each and every life -- even before our birth. You and I were created to be His forever child.

What more proof could we need that God genuinely loves each of us than realizing He dealt with each of us as a separate, individual in determining the where and when each of us would live and the talents we each would have? Because you live, it proves God's love of you.

God knew when and where we needed to live and what lessons He needed us to learn by having our specific families. He chose the time and place we would be born and live so we would reach out to find Him and serve Him. The many obstacles we may need to overcome are for our spiritual development as we learn to trust and rely on Him.

Once Noah and his family were sealed inside the ark, everyone else on earth was destroyed. So obviously, those living today, those who lived before us, and those who will live after us came from Adam and then from one of Noah's sons, either from Japheth, Shem, or Ham. Noah's son Japheth had seven sons; Shem had five; Ham four (Ge. 10). Researchers have studied where these men settled, and most agree on the following locations.

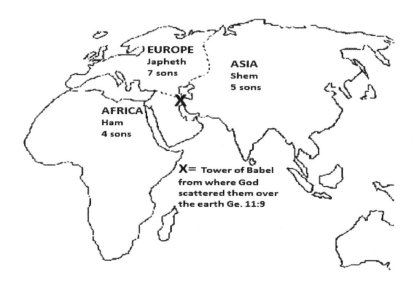

Noah was the tenth descendant of Adam, coming through Adam's son Seth. God gave Noah the same instructions He had given Adam and Eve. They were to be fruitful, increase in number, and fill the earth (Ge. 9:1). It was another opportunity for men to do what's right by worshipping only the Lord.

Before Noah entered the ark, God promised to establish a Covenant with him (Ge. 6:18). After the flood, God made a Covenant between Himself and the earth (Ge. 9: 14), and He said it was a Covenant for all generations to come. He promised never again to curse the ground, even though man's inclination of his heart is evil from childhood (Ge. 8: 20-21). God's Covenant is binding until the end of time. His promise is unconditional. No matter how wicked mankind becomes, God will never again flood the entire world. However, had

God not made the rainbow, all might have again been destroyed by water because, as the number of men increased, once again, they became increasingly evil. But no matter how men act, God always keeps His promise. *Whenever the rainbow appears in the clouds, I will see it and remember the everlasting Covenant between God and all living creatures of every kind on the earth* (Ge. 9:16).

In addition, God now allowed people to eat meat: *everything that lives and moves will be food for you., just as I gave you the green plants, I now give you everything* (Ge. 9:3). God put fear of men on all the beasts of the earth, all the birds of the air, upon every creature that moved along the ground, and fish of the sea (v. 2), but God did forewarn that He would demand an accounting of lifeblood. Even today, God keeps count of every sparrow that dies (Mt. 10:29). The only restriction was that men were not to eat meat that had its lifeblood still in it (Ge. 9:4). Blood was to be drained from the animal before being cooked.

God gave Noah instructions on how to punish someone who murdered another. Whoever sheds the blood of man, by man shall his blood be shed; for in the image of God had God made man (Ge. 9:6). Anyone who kills another is accountable to God (v.5). This death sentence for a murderer was given by the Lord years before the law was given Moses.

Man had another opportunity to create a good world. However, it is fortunate that God's Covenant did not require a commitment of faithfulness from Noah and his sons, because it wasn't long until they sinned. Noah drank wine from his vineyard, became drunk, and lay naked in his tent. Ham saw his father and instead of covering his father to hide his father's nakedness, he laughed and told his bothers. Shem and Japheth walked backwards into the tent, with faces turned the other way to cover their father's nakedness.

Remember how the shame of nakedness was the natural reaction of Adam and Eve when they sinned. Once Noah was sober, and learned what his youngest child had done, Noah's shame and wrath was displayed on Ham's son, Canaan. Noah pronounced a strong curse on Canaan (Ge. 9:24).

Noah told the children of Japheth and Shem they could intermarry and for their children to live together, but they were never to intermarry and have children with Ham's offspring (9:27). Ham and his children were to be his brother's slaves.

The part that deeply distressed Noah was that Ham's and Canaan's sin was sexual. There is debate about what may have transpired in this scene. In some Biblical versions, the phrase uncover nakedness is reworded as "have sexual relations with" as in Leviticus (18:6, 17, 19 KJ). Some think Ham or

Canaan may have engaged in some kind of sexual activity or dishonored Noah's private parts. Whatever they did, it was wicked enough to incite Noah's wrath.

It was through Ham's son Canaan and Canaan's many children, that many idolatrous clans came and fought the Israelites (Ge. 10: 15). They also established the wicked cities of Sodom and Gomorrah (Ge. 10:20) that God later destroyed.

Imagine God's fury today, as He watches men and women openly displaying their nakedness. Even in many churches, more flesh is paraded than one's best clothing to honor the Lord. After publishing an article on modesty in Christian Woman Magazine, one grandmother threatened me with physical harm if I ever mentioned modesty again. That same day, my husband and I watched as her granddaughters attempted to roll up their short shorts even higher for worship service. Still, several congregations asked permission to print the article to insert in their weekly handouts.

Rather than spreading out to live in multiple areas as God commanded, Noah and his sons remained together and spoke one language. The men decided, *"Come, let's make bricks and bake them thoroughly. Let us build ourselves a city, with a tower that reaches to the heavens, so that we many make a name for ourselves and not be scattered over the face of the whole world"* (Ge. 11:3). How quickly they ignored they were to be faithful, migrate, and replenish the entire earth.

Recall how Adam and Eve chose to eat the forbidden fruit in hope of being wise in their own eyes, rather than being dependent on God. Likewise, when Noah's family planned to build the tower of Babel to heaven, it wasn't to honor God, but to honor themselves. People have always craved notoriety for what they do, know, and have, not credit the Lord for their accomplishments. Since the days of Adam and Eve, pride has been one of the dominant strategies Satan successfully uses to have people sin. How we humans crave praise and having others think us smart and talented.

When the Lord saw men's desire to make a name for themselves, rather than being God's spokesperson for teaching their children and future generations about Him, the Lord ruined their plans. He said, *"If as one person speaking the same language, they have begun to do this, then nothing they plan to do will be impossible for them. Come, let us go down and confuse their language so they will not understand each other"* (Ge. 11:6-7). Imagine all they could have done if they had been working together to honor the Lord and not themselves.

When they no longer understood each other, they stopped building, and the Lord scattered them all over the earth. Noah, like Adam, sinned in his new world.

God has always condemned behaviors that cause people to miss having an eternal relationship with Him. *"The Lord is not slack concerning his promise, as some men count slackness; but is longsuffering to us-ward, not willing that any should perish, but that all should come to repentance"* (2 Pe. 3:9).

God has always condemned behaviors that cause people to miss having an eternal relationship with Him

If you want to know the Lord, study Genesis, know what disappoints God, learn why and how He makes promises, and how He addresses disobedience. Jesus is the same yesterday, today, and tomorrow, so if He hated something in Genesis, we need to study to learn if it's okay to do it today. If He required something in Genesis, we need to learn if our New Covenant changed the old requirement or if it's still binding. And many of the same requirements are in both the Old and New Testaments. Genesis definitely shares much of the Lord's one-on-one interactions with mankind, as He sends angels or comes Himself to bring men messages from the Father, and how Jesus took on various forms to meet with them.

Best of all, Genesis reveals that, no matter how angry God became with men, He continued caring for them by raising up a believing man to lead them back on course. From the very beginning, God remained committed to fulfilling heaven's salvation plan for mankind. No matter how sinful mankind became, God continued making Covenanted promises that would allow us to live eternally with Him.

FAITH = RIGHTEOUSNESS

A bram (later renamed Abraham) was the tenth-generation patriarch from Noah, coming through Noah's son, Shem. Noah lived 350 years after the flood, Shem 500 years. People born before the flood lived hundreds of years, those born afterwards no longer did. Abraham's life was shorter: *This is the sum of the years of Abraham's life which he lived: one hundred and seventy-five years* (Gen 25:7). For 39 years, all three men were alive at the same time, and Abram would have known Noah's great-great-grandson, Eber. This helps explain how Abraham, who was reared in a culture of idol worship, knew it was God who called him to leave a place called Haran. These elderly men served as the link for Abraham retaining belief in the true God. Scripture calls Eber the founder of the Hebrew race, and Abraham was called a Hebrew (Ge. 14:13; Nu. 24:24). Perhaps, it was Eber who taught Abraham about the Lord.

After the flood, it wasn't long until men who knew God glorified Him not as God, and exchanged the glory of the God for images made to look like mortal man or animals (Ro. 1:22-23). Jewish history says Abraham's father, Terah, sold idols for a living. Scripture reveals that *Terah, the father of Abraham,*

Nahor, and Haran (deceased father of Lot) lived beyond the River and worshiped other Gods (Jos. 24:3). Terah took Abraham and his wife Sarah, his son, Nahor, and grandson, Lot, and settled in Haran with plans to go onto the land called Canaan. It was there that God called to Abraham to leave his country, his people, his father's household, and go where God would tell him. Abraham immediately left. *By faith, Abraham when called to go out to a place he would later receive as an inheritance, he obeyed and went* (Heb. 11:8).

What's remarkable is Abraham went, not knowing where he was to go. By faith, he went to live in the land of promise, as in a foreign land. He lived in tents as did Isaac, his son, and Jacob, his grandson. They were heirs with him of God's promise. Abraham went because He was looking for the city that has foundations, whose designer and builder is God (Heb. 11:8-10).

Five times God made Abraham promises (Ge. 12:1-3; 15:1-6; 15:18; 22:13-18; 17:15-21). Abraham was a man of great faith (Heb. 11:8-19; Gal 3:6-9). He became the physical and spiritual father of the Jewish race (Jn. 8:31-33, 39, 53; Ac. 7:2). Later, he was called the spiritual father of all Jews and all Gentile believers (Ro. 4:11-12). God told him, "**all** *nations will be blessed by you*" (Gen. 12:3; Gal. 3:8).

God's Covenant with Abraham had four promises: land where Canaanites lived, but it would be several generations before his family owned it (Jos. 22:1-6); descendants as many as the stars and sand who would bless the whole earth (Ge. 22:17-18); his descendants would become a great nation with a mighty king (17:6); and God would bring blessings and redemption to all people through his people. God promised: I will make you into a great nation and will bless you; make your name great, and you will be a blessing; I will bless those who bless you and curse those who curse you, and all on earth will be blessed through you (Ge. 12:2-3). The evil Canaanite people had divided into many groups, but all were through sons of Ham, grandsons of Noah. They occupied the promised land, that God swore to Abraham, *"To your offspring I will give this land"* (v.7).

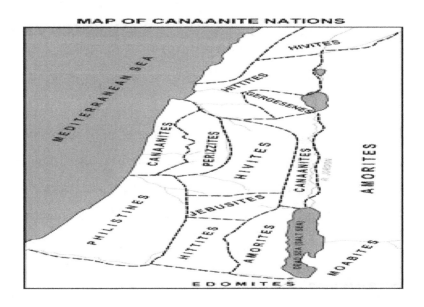

Later, God's promise was confirmed with Abraham's son, Isaac, (Ge. 21:12; 26:3-4) and then with his grandson Jacob (Ge. 28: 14-15).

Paul explained the importance of Abraham was his being the father of God's unconditional Covenant promise of grace, for all who obey. *Therefore, the **promise comes** by faith, so that it may be **by grace and may be guaranteed to all** of Abraham's offspring -- not only to those who are of the law but also to those **who are of the faith of Abraham**. Abraham believed God, and it was counted unto him for righteousness* (Ro. 4:3 my emphasis).

The blessing of Abraham was also for Gentiles (Gal. 3:14). *The Covenant promises were spoken to Abraham and to his seed.* That seed was Christ who came through Abraham's lineage

(Gal. 3:16). *Jesus redeemed us in order that the blessing given to Abraham might come to the Gentiles through Christ Jesus, so that by faith we might receive the promise of the Spirit* (Gal. 3;14). Righteousness from God comes through faith in Jesus Christ to **all who believe and obey**.

Even with such promises, Abraham experienced struggles with his faith. First, he did not fully obey by leaving his father's family. Lot went with him, and problems arose because of Lot.

Second, because of their advanced ages, Abraham doubted his and Sarah's ability to have a son as God promised. He asked God to let his ancestry promise come through his servant boy. God refused. Once when God said Sarah would have a son, she laughed. Then she denied laughing (Ge. 18:12-15). Another time Abraham also laughed. Still, God kept promising them a son.

Third, Sarah continued to doubt the Lord's promise until it impacted Abraham's faith. Sarah asked Abraham to have a child with her servant girl, Hagar, and Abraham agreed. Hagar was an Egyptian from Ham's ancestry; the people God had forbidden Shem's family to intermarry (Ge. 21:8-21). Abraham had a son, Ishmael, by Hagar, and he asked the Lord to let Ishmael be the son of promise. The Lord refused, and avowed Sarah was to have a son named Isaac. After Isaac was born, Ishmael created conflict by taunting young Isaac, and God told Abraham to send Ishmael away. He left with a blessing from the Lord. God described Ishmael as a wild donkey of a man who would live fighting all his kinsmen.

Fourth, Abraham asked Sarah to lie twice: to Pharaoh (Ge. 12:10-20 and to Abimelech (20: 1-18), saying she was his sister. He feared being killed so they could marry her. The lie was a half-truth; they had the same father (20:12). However, they failed to realize that when the Lord asked them to do something, He would protect them and didn't need their help.

When God reminded Abraham how plentiful his ancestry would be and all the land he would possess, Abraham asked for proof. God confirmed it with a Covenant ceremony that required blood.

According to Compelling Truth, a traditional way of making a Covenant was with the use of animal blood to seal a Covenant. If the pledge was unconditional, it was binding on only one party, with no conditions required of the other person. Such was God vowing to keep a promise to Abraham of land and many descendants. Most often God made an unconditional Covenant with a man, but a conditional Covenant with the people. God promised special blessings to the people provided they fulfilled certain conditions. When they disobeyed, they were punished as they knew in advance to expect.

Before sealing the Covenant with Abraham, God caused Abraham to fall into a deep sleep and explained to Abraham that his offspring would live 400 years in Egypt as mistreated slaves. He told Abraham the nation they served would be punished, and in the fourth generation his descendants would return. Their delayed leaving was because, as yet, the sins of the Amorites had not reached it full measure (Ge. 15:16). Children through Noah - Ham - Canaan, called Amorites, were the most wicked. They were depraved beyond redemption (Ge. 15:16; Lev. 18:21). They practiced child sacrifice to their gods (Dt. 12:30), incest, bestiality, shrine prostitution (Ge. 38:21), and worshipped multiple gods. Still, they were not as evil as they would become. Later, God's people would destroy them. Plus, we know that at this time, the Israelites were not prepared to leave Egypt because years later, when Moses attempted to lead them from slavery in Egypt, they often argued with him and grumbled, begging to return. Both the Israelites and Amorites would be ready - but later.

The Lord had Abraham bring a heifer, goat, ram, dove, and pigeon. He cut the heifer, goat, and ram into two pieces, laid each half facing its opposite half, leaving a bloody walkway between them (Ge. 15:8-11). Once dark, and Abraham was asleep again, Jesus sealed the Covenant by appearing in the form of a smoking firepot, with a blazing torch. He passed between the animal halves among their blood. This ceremony signified the bonding of God's unconditional Covenant of land with Abraham.

God proved that with Him a person's age does not matter, for He kept His promise, and Isaac, the child of promise, was born through 90-year-old Sarah. Abraham's offspring would become such large nations that God would later divide the Promised Land among twelve men of Abraham's ancestry.

The original Covenant had included only Abraham and Sarah. Nothing was required of their servants, many of whom had been purchased from clans who worshipped other gods. When Abraham was 99 years old God required that all males born in Abraham's house and those he purchased, who were eight days old, were to be circumcised. *"You shall be circumcised in the flesh of your foreskin, and it shall be the sign of the Covenant between Me and you.* (Ge. 17:9-11). Unlike the animal blood of the Covenant with Abraham, this Covenant was sealed in the blood of their own flesh. This duty-bound all in Abraham's care to the Lord and showed that God expected everyone in their group to worship only Him. Anyone not circumcised was to be cut off from his people, for breaking the Covenant. Abraham and Ishmael were circumcised that day.

Abraham's circumcision was a **sign of the righteousness that he had by faith while he was still uncircumcised** (Ro. 4:10-11 my emphasis). His promise of being heir of the world came through **righteousness that comes by faith** (v. 13 my emphasis). All believers (then and today) are children of Abraham (Gal. 3:7). **In Christ, you are circumcised** in the putting off of the sinful nature, not with circumcision done by hands of men, but with circumcision done **by Christ's blood, having been buried with Him in baptism and raised with Him through your faith** in the power of God who raised Him from the dead (Col. 2:11-12 my emphasis).

A significant time in Abraham's life was when Jesus took the form of a human man, and He and two other men (angels) appeared to Abraham and ate with him. The Lord decided to share with Abraham that He was there because of the outcry from Sodom. Scripture says Jesus shared this with him because He knew Abraham would *direct his children and his household after him to keep the way of the Lord* by doing what is right and just, so that the Lord would bring about for Abraham what He had promised (Ge. 18:19). With Jesus restating the Covenant promises, it appears this was a

Covenant celebration. Three times in Scripture, Abraham is called God's friend (2 Chron. 20:7; Isa. 41:8; Jas. 2:23).

Jesus shared his reason with Abraham because He knew Abraham would direct his children and his household after him to keep the way of the Lord

Abraham trusted the Lord, and likewise, the Lord trusted Abraham to do all He asked. Jesus even allowed Abraham to negotiate the number of good people that would stop His destroying Sodom. Abraham was concerned because Lot, his nephew, lived there.

God had told Abraham to leave his family's household because He foreknew the burden Lot would become. During a war, Lot was captured and Abraham had to help save him. In addition, Lot had obviously failed to teach his daughters about the Lord and apparently didn't care they were prepared to marry men of the wicked city of Sodom. In fact, we know nothing of Lot being married until he moved to Sodom. It may be that his wife was reared there. If so, it helps explain why she looked back as Sodom was burning. Perhaps, she was missing and worrying about her relatives and friends. If Lot had taught his daughters about the true God, surley they would not have wanted to have children with him. Lot's faith did not support his uncle Abraham and caused Abraham problems.

The genuineness of Abraham's faith was revealed in the patriarch's willingness to sacrifice his only son, Isaac, because after Isaac's birth by his elderly wife, he believed all that God had promised. Isaac's birth removed his every doubt. (Gen. 22:1-19). By faith Abraham, when **his faith was tested**, offered up Isaac, his son. He proved he was willing to offer his only son, of whom it was said, *Through Isaac shall your offspring be named.* Abraham knew God would keep His Covenant promise by using Isaac. Therefore, he believed if he sacrificed his son that God would raise Isaac from the dead, from which, figuratively, he did receive him back (Heb. 11:8-10, 17-19). Instead of him having to kill his son, God intervened and substituted a ram.

What's interesting about Abraham's sacrifice is the similarities of Abraham's sacrifice of his only son to the sacrifice of the Holy Father's only Son, Jesus Christ. It's as if mankind was being offered a preview of what was to come with Christ.

With such a proven record of faith, Abraham is called our father of faith. Abraham believed God, and it was credited to him as righteousness. All who believe are children of Abraham, including Gentiles. The Scripture foresaw that God would justify Gentiles by their faith, and announced the gospel in advance to Abraham: ***All nations*** *will be blessed* *through you. So those **who have faith are blessed along with Abraham**, the man of faith* (Gal. 3: 6-9 my emphasis). And that's you and me.

Paul defined gospel, the same as Abraham had been told: *The power of God for the salvation of everyone who believes; first to the Jew, then for the Gentile. It is written: The **righteous will live by faith*** (Ro. 1: 16-17 my emphasis). Abraham responded as he did, because he was looking forward to the city with foundations, whose architect and builder is God (Heb.11: 10). He wanted to live eternally with God. Abraham was righteous, because no matter what God asked him to do, he responded immediately from faith. God asks for the same faith from us.

Early doubts of Abraham and Sarah appeared to be due to them being so elderly. Each time the promise of them having a son was discussed, they mentioned their ages. Abraham was old, and Sarah was past a woman's physical ability to get pregnant. They both thought about the current condition of an aged bodies rather remembering the Lord had created their bodies. The older they grew, the funnier such an idea seemed. Nothing in their experiences gave them reason to think it was possible. What they ignored was that with the Creator of mankind all things are possible. They had forgotten this. How often we do the same.

I can identify with Sarah for I too wanted a child and was told I should not have another. I had two sons, but that didn't keep me from wanting a daughter. With God's help, I overcame numerous obstacles. I traveled to Memphis to hear a man speak who was in charge of Lubbock Texas Home for Unwed Mothers. Although the speaker agreed to give me the contact person's name, he told me it was impossible to adopt out of state. Likewise, the contact gave me no hope, but she let us complete the application forms. After their approval, she insisted Arkansas had to interview us. Only Arkansas refused, saying they did not have time to do work for another state. By accident (or as I believe - by God's plan), my son became ill and while with his doctor, I told him about our hope of adopting a daughter from Texas. He took my information, met with our Governor that week, and the Governor asked Arkansas Social Services to interview us and complete the adoption. Then I had surgery and could not travel to get her until she was 10 days old. Those 10 days seems an eternity, but what joy when she was placed in my arms. And how thrilled the boys were, brothers who had spent hours praying for her and who selected her name. The younger son was not yet in school, and for weeks, multiple times each day, he came bolting through the door yelling, "Me check me baby, Mama." He would pat her and race back out to play.

Unlike, poor Sarah who could not tolerate Hagar's son taunting Isaac, my daughter was blessed with brothers who cherished their new, perfect little sister. For years, any time she wasn't feeling well, she would lay her head in the boys' laps and beg, "Tell me, me story, Brubber." She was asking them to explain how we adopted her. No one will be able to convince me that getting her wasn't by God's intervention. . . just as it was with Sarah having Isaac.

Our Savior, Jesus Christ, would be a descendant of Abraham, the Father of all nations. Abraham's strong faith is so powerfully important because he became the father of both Jews and Gentiles who believe in our Messiah, Jesus Christ. I am so thankful the promise included us.

BLESSING OF FORGIVENESS

Abraham's Canaanite neighbors were unacceptable as a wife for his son Isaac. Finding the right wife was necessary for God's promise of numerous descendants coming through Abraham to further God's work on earth. Abraham sent his trusted servant to find Isaac a wife from the household of his brother, Nahor. The servant's faithful prayer ensured he found Rebekah, and that she agreed to go back with him to marry Isaac. When Isaac was 40 years old, he took Rebekah into his mother's tent, married her, and he loved her. So, Isaac was comforted after his mother's death (Ge. 24:6-7).

When a famine broke out, Isaac went to Abimelech king of the Philistines, and the Lord met him telling him not to go to Egypt, but to stay in the land where he was. It was then that God confirmed on oath with him the same Covenant promise He had made to Abraham. God told Isaac the Covenant with him was because his father, Abraham, had obeyed and kept His commands, decrees, and laws (Ge. 26: 1-6).

After years of Isaac and Rebekah not having a child, Isaac prayed to the Lord, and God gave them twins. The Lord told Rebekah that she carried two nations in her womb who would be separated, with one stronger than the other, and the older would serve the younger (Ge. 25:23). Their twin sons were called Esau, the first-born, and Jacob. The boys were very different in interest, morals, and looks. Isaac favored Esau because he was an outdoors man; Sarah preferred Jacob because he was a homebody. Such partiality set up discord and deception among the parents, something that always negatively influences their children.

For example, as Isaac lay dying, he was almost blind. He called for his sons to give them a blessing and asked Esau to go kill wild game and prepare a meal he liked. Rebekah overheard Isaac's request and wanted the blessing to go to her favored Jacob. She helped Jacob prepare a meal and dress in Esau clothes to deceive Isaac into giving the blessing to Jacob.

In essence, she told her son to lie to his father, and it worked. Jacob received Isaac's blessing and the family birthright that was supposed to go to the older son. Receiving a blessing from one's father was a high honor, and losing the blessing was equal to a family curse. However, Isaac did not know that years earlier, his favored son, Esau, while extremely hungry, had sold his birthright to Jacob for a bowl of stew. Because he did this, Scripture says, Esau despised his birthright (Ge. 25:32-34). Hebrews (12:16) described: *See that no one is sexually immoral, or is godless like Esau, who for a single meal sold his inheritance rights as the oldest son.*

The blessing Isaac unknowingly gave to his younger son, Jacob, gave him the earth's bounty and authority over his brother (Ge, 17: 29-29). It promised that those who blessed Jacob would be blessed and cursed if he was cursed. The words were similar to God's promise to Abraham (Ge. 12: 3). Learning of this, Esau became distraught and pleaded, *"Have you not reserved a blessing for me?"* (Ge. 27:34-38). Isaac prophesied that Esau would one day rebel against Jacob's rule (vs. 39-40).

In addition, Esau had committed spiritual adultery against God by marrying a Canaanite who worshipped idols. Malachi (1:3) states that God hated Esau. There was nothing morally good about Esau. He had no interest in being the faithful spiritual leader that God needed for the pure bloodline through which Jesus would come.

When Esau learned his firstborn blessing was given to his brother, he became so angry he threatened to kill Jacob. Learning Esau vowed to kill Jacob, Rebekah pleaded with Isaac to send Jacob to Haran to find a wife from among their family of Laban (Ge. 27, 28). Her plan worked because they did not want him to marry a woman from forbidden clans as Esau had done her plan worked.

As Jacob traveled to Haran, he had a vision where he saw angels ascending and descending on a ladder. In Jacob's dream, the Lord promised him the land about him and numerous offspring (Ge. 28:10-15). God blessed Jacob saying, *"I am the God of your father Abraham. Do not be afraid, for I am with you: I will bless you and will increase the number of your descendants for the sake of my servant Abraham."* He received the Covenant promise from God that was originally given to Abraham and Isaac.

In Haran, Jacob worked years to have Rachel become his wife, only to be deceived by his father-in-law and find he had married her sister Leah. Jacob loved Rachel enough to continue working a total of 14 years to marry her.

Finally, Jacob decided he had served his father-in-law long enough, as he had made them both very rich. He made plans to return to his father's homeland of Canaan, taking all his possessions, children, and wives with him.

An angel of God met Jacob, as he was struggling with how to deal with his brother Esau. Jacob sent all his family and possessions across the river. As he was alone that night, a man (Jesus) wrestled with him till daybreak. When the man saw he could not overpower Jacob, he touched the socket of Jacob's hip, and his hip was twisted. Jacob was committed to treating Esau properly and nothing Jesus tested him with changed his mind. Having to spend the rest of his life walking with a limp ensured he remembered his commitment, and it made him seem less of a threat to Esau. The man asked Jacob to let him go, but Jacob refused until he was given a blessing. The man said, *"Your name will no longer be Jacob, but Israel, because you have struggled with God and with men and have overcome."* Later, all who followed with Jacob were called Israelites. We know this was Jesus because angels do determine men's names.

Jesus had helped Jacob wrestle with ways he might make amends with his brother so they could live in peace (Ge. 32:22-32). Without doing so, Jacob would return home fearing that Esau's earlier death threat would become a reality.

Jacob was a man of spiritual morals and a kind heart. Jacob knew he and his mother had wronged Esau, and to live near him would be best for all if they could live peacefully. After the night of struggling with God, Jacob chose to make amends by treating Esau as if Esau had been given his father's blessing, that by birth order, he rightly deserved. Jesus had tested Jacob's heart to prove he was fully committed to do what was right. Jacob returned to Esau what rightly by birth order belong to him.

However, doing so, required serious sacrifice by Jacob. The son who received the paternal blessing inherited a double portion of assets and assumed the role of head of the family once the father died (Dt. 21:15-17). After wrestling with Jesus,

Jacob was prepared to sacrifice all this. He had a good heart and knew he could trust the Lord to care for him for doing so.

When Jacob's messengers met Esau, they called Esau lord and told Esau that his servant Jacob was coming. Jacob had all his wives and children bow to Esau, and Jacob bowed several times when he saw his brother. Esau ran to meet him. Esau embraced Jacob, threw his arms around his neck and kissed him. Together they wept (Ge. 33: 4). God blessed Jacob for how he treated Esau, and Jacob's decision bonded the brother's relationship.

Jacob provided a great lesson for learning how to make amends with another we have wronged. He restored to Esau the father's firstborn blessing by treating Esau as if their father had actually given it to him. Jacob's addressing Esau as his lord proved Jacob's sincerity.

Still, Jesus would not come through Esau because of his evil decisions. Instead, Jacob was given this honor. Jacob could surely be called a peacemaker, like Matthew (5:7) called peacemakers sons of God.

God forgives our past sins through the blood of His Son, but how we forgive others is a condition of our service to the Lord. The command to forgive is more stringent when it is a

Christian dealing with another Christian. Jesus taught we must place forgiveness of a brother as more important than our worship of Him. He taught: *If you are offering your gift at the altar and there remember that your brother has something against you, leave your gift there in front of the altar. First, go and be reconciled to your brother; then, come and offer your gift* (Mt. 5:23-24).

Paul said it slightly different: *As God's chosen people, holy and dearly loved, clothe yourselves with compassion, kindness, humility, gentleness and patience. Bear with each other and forgive whatever grievances you may have against one another. Forgive as the Lord forgave you* (Col. 3:12-13). We must remember that Christ, being weighted down with my sins and your sins on the cross, is an example of forgiveness that we can never match. Nor will our doing so hurt as deeply as our sin pained Christ.

Scripture says it is impossible to avoid being offended, and Jesus said that mistreatments will come. *Things that cause people to sin are bound to come, **but woe to that person through whom they come*** (Lk. 17:1 my emphasis). No one goes through life without being insulted or criticized, some are even abused or tortured, and each situation can tempt us to sin. Read Luke 17:1 bold words again. The word woe is defined as anguish, affliction, or grief. God is telling us that misery inflicts the offensive person. Perhaps, Jacob's woe was his being tricked into marrying a woman he didn't love and then having to work additional years for his true love. Jacob had obviously wrestled with God about wronging his brother. Now that he was coming home to live, the Lord ensured he addressed how he could correct mistreatment of Esau.

We must remember that God promises it will be bad for one who offends us. He will suffer for doing us wrong. We can let it go, knowing God will deal justly with that person, and knowing God promises us glory for overlooking the issue (Prov. 19:11). Once Jacob decided to do what was right, he knew he and Esau could live in peace without fearing each other. And Jacob retained the glory of Jesus becoming his heir.

Granted there is a big difference between letting go of bitterness toward a person insulting us, and being mistreated sexually as Noah's sons mistreated him. Certainly, we are not to put ourselves in a vulnerable position of being with another who has done us serious harm and denies doing the wrong.

Denying what they have done, shows they have no regret, and proves they have not changed. Recall the story of Joseph, a strong man of God, who multiple times seriously tested his brothers before risking to trust them again. Only when Joseph's brothers admitted how wrongly they had mistreated him, did he tell them who he was.

Still, even if we must go our separate ways and never see each other again, forgiveness makes it easier to see the love of the Lord as He continues to work in our lives. It is us, whom God blesses with peace and joy once we refuse to dwell on the painful situation. How relieved Esau was to know things were made right for him as the firstborn son. With great joy, he welcomed his brother Jacob home.

Jacob was blessed as Paul stressed: so that he was not outwitted by Satan. He ensured Satan could not control his thoughts and take advantage of him. As Paul pointed out, Jacob was not ignorant of Satan's schemes (2 Cor. 2:11).

God demands that we forgive so we keep Satan from using our emotions to tempt us and for our own peace of mind so we can concentrate on pleasing the Lord. Continually thinking about the way another pained us, takes our time and energy away from the Lord. We are to be self-controlled and keep our minds clear so we can pray (1 Pe. 4:7).

God promises to forgive us as we forgive others, because without forgiving we leave no mental space to focus on Him. If pain and mistreatment dominate our thoughts, without realizing, we can make our offender our idol, by giving him mental and emotional energy that rightly belongs to God. No one, no matter how they have wronged us, is worth our spending eternity in hell.

When we pray as we should, God responds. With every temptation to dwell on the mistreatment, God promises to help. We can immediately stop and pray, admit our temptation to dwell on the situation, and ask God to replace it with better thoughts. Otherwise, God may test us and leave us wrestling with the situation all night as Jacob did. Every time we think of a mistreatment, we can ask the Lord to replace it with good thoughts until we no longer recall it. Forgiving gives us spiritual, mental, and emotional freedom, and it restores our relationship with the Lord so we are again praying as we should.

Abraham, Isaac, and Jacob lived by faith. They did not receive what God promised, but they knew it would happen and they clung to God's promise. By faith Isaac blessed Jacob and Esau. By faith Jacob, when he was dying blessed each of Joseph's sons. By faith Joseph, when his end was near, spoke about the exodus of the Israelites from Egypt, and knew with God having said that it would happen then it would. He proved his faith by telling them to take his bones with them when they left (Heb. 11:20-22).

Those with such faith today have an even better promise. *God had planned something better for us so that only together with us would they be made perfect* (Heb. 11:40). Think about the last sentence. Only with you and with me will these great and faithful believers receive something better. Wow! Cling to God's promises. The best is yet to be.

ARGUING WITH GOD

G od had told Abraham that for years his ancestors would be treated as slaves, and when they left their captors, they would leave with great riches. This happened through Abraham's grandson, Israel, formerly called Jacob. Israel would become known as the father of the Tribes of Israel.

Israel (formerly Jacob) repeated a parenting style of his parents, Isaac and Rebekah, by showing preferential treatment to his favored son, Joseph. Such differences created deep resentment among Israel's other sons. They disliked Joseph so strongly that, when presented with an opportunity, they sold him to a caravan of Ishmaelite's, a clan of Abraham's son by Hagar. The Ishmaelites sold Joseph in Egypt. The brothers dipped Joseph's coat in goat's blood to have their father think Joseph was dead.

In Egypt, God blessed Joseph, and he prospered, as did those he served. Joseph was put in charge of Potiphar's household and all that he owned (Ge. 39:2-5). However, Potiphar's wife asked Joseph to go to bed with her. He refused, saying he could not do such a wicked thing and sin against the Lord. Leaving his cloak as he fled, she lied and reported that he had sexually attacked her. Joseph was put in prison, but Joseph's goodness gained him favor of the warden, and he was put in charge.

Later, Joseph was able to interpret Pharaoh's dream, and ultimately at age 31, he was made second in command of Egypt (Ge. 41:40-41). Pharaoh dreamed of Egypt having seven years of plenty and seven years of famine. Joseph was charged with storing food during the good years so they had plenty in the lean years.

The famine spread to where Joseph's father, Israel, and his brothers lived, and his brothers traveled to Egypt to buy food. Because he had aged and Joseph dressed and spoke as an Egyptian, the brothers did not recognize him. He was able to severely test them multiple times, to ensure they had changed. Once convinced they were different, Joseph gained Pharaoh's permission to move his family to Egypt. Israel went to live in Egypt with his son Joseph in the land of Ham, youngest son of Noah, the son God condemned intermarrying with (Ps. 78:51,105:23, 27, 106:22). And interest note is when God killed the firstborn in Egypt, the chief of Egypt's strength was in the firstfruits of manhood (the oldest) in the tents of Ham (78:51).

After their father, Israel, died, Joseph's brothers feared he might hold a grudge against them for having sold him to the Ishmaelites. The brothers came to Joseph, threw themselves down before him, and called themselves Joseph's slaves.

Joseph responded with, *"You intended to harm me, but God intended it for good to accomplish what is now being done, the saving of many lives. Don't be afraid. I will provide for you and your children"* (Ge. 50: 15-21).

His bothers provide a powerful example of how to humbly seek forgiveness when we have wronged another. Likewise, it's how we are to forgive another when he admits his wrong, and proves he has changed.

After Joseph and all his family had died, the Israelites continued living in Egypt. It was a land of idol worship where Ham, and his offspring had multiplied, and many Israelites had adopted their worship ways. The Israelites multiplied greatly, and the land filled with them (Ex 1:6-7).

When a new ruler, who had not known Joseph, came to power, he feared the Israelites might join Egypt's enemies if a war broke out. To control the Israelites, he assigned slave masters to oppress them with forced labor. Still, the more the Israelites were oppressed, the more they multiplied (Ex. 1: 8-14).

Years later, God chose Moses to lead the Israelites from their bondage in Egypt, so He could fulfill His Covenant promise to Abraham, Isaac, and Jacob. But first, Moses had to meet God. As Moses led his flock, an angel appeared in a bush that was on fire but was not being consumed. Moses went to inspect it. God called from within the bush for Moses to remove his sandals. God wanted him to know that His presence made even dirt holy.

God told Moses He had heard the cry of His people and was sending him to bring the Israelites out of Egypt. When Moses asked His name, God answered, "I AM." Tell the Israelites, I AM, the God of Abraham, Isaac, and Jacob has sent Me to you. (Ex. 3:1-11). Moses kept insisting he could not speak well enough, and God gave him Aaron as a helper.

Most know the story of how God, through Moses, brought harsh plagues on the Egyptians. After the last plague, that took the life of every first born in Egypt that didn't have blood on their door posts, the Israelites were allowed to leave Egypt. Under the direction of Moses and Aaron, Jesus led the people by a cloud during the day, by fire at night and provided all their needs.

It's estimated that the number of mature Israelite men leaving Egypt was 600,000 (Ex. 12:37), plus the 23,000 Levites (Num.3:39). To this, must be added the converts (Ex. 12:38), women, and children. The estimated total is approximately two to two and half million people. The number is provided to understand the challenge Moses faced in keeping this many people obedient.

Three months after the Israelites were freed from slavery, they arrived in the land of Horeb at the base of Mount Sinai (Ex. 19:1). God called Moses up the mountain and gave him the terms of a Covenant. He promised if the people would keep the Covenant, they would be His special people, a kingdom of priests, and a holy nation. The people accepted God's terms.

To ensure the people believed Moses, the Lord (Jesus) wanted to speak so the people could hear Him. Moses consecrated the people by having them wash their clothes and abstain from sex. They needed to cleanse themselves of sin with the use of water and concentrate on their relationship with Him, not come with thoughts of each other. Note the similarities to our being baptized to wash away our sins and putting God first.

The people were instructed not to come near or touch the mountain or they would die. Moses spoke, and the voice of God answered as a sound of a trumpet blast grew louder and louder. They watched as thunder and lightning bolted across the sky, and the mountain trembled violently (Ex. 19: 14-19). Moses explained that God was **testing them so their fear of Him would keep them from sinning** (Ex. 20:20 my emphasis).

Moses went up the mountain, and God spoke the Ten Commandments to him, as Moses wrote the words. Seeing the mountain covered in smoke, the people stayed back a safe distance for fear they would die. Moses told the people that God had spoken to him from heaven, and they were not to make themselves gods of silver or gold (v. 23).

The people agreed with God's requirements: *"Everything the Lord has said we will do."* However, they broke their commitment, and animal blood sacrifices were introduced as a way to forgive their sins. Moses built an altar and set up 12 stone pillars, representing the twelve tribes of Israel. They sacrificed bulls, and Moses put half the blood in a bowl. The other half, he sprinkled on the altar. He read the Covenant to the people, and with their commitment to obey, he sprinkled the bowl of blood on them (Ex. 24:1-8). This sealed the Covenant. They needed purification with blood to confirm their Covenant agreement, just as God used animal blood with Adam and Abraham, and we need Jesus' blood with the New Covenant.

Moses, Aaron, Nadab, Abihu, and seventy elders went up Mount Sinai and had a meal with Jesus to celebrate the confirmation of the Covenant agreements (Ex. 24:1-10). Note it is similar to how today's church celebrates the New Covenant with the Lord's Supper. We are not told what form Jesus took, but we know no one could see His spiritual face and live. Jesus called Moses higher up the mountain. He stayed 40 days while receiving the Ten Commandments, written on stone by God's own hand (Ex. 24:7-8; Heb 9:17-20). God gave him directions for the tabernacle and priests. A cloud covered the mountain, and the glory of the Lord settled on Mount Sinai. To the people, the glory of God glowed like the mountain was a consuming fire (Ex. 24:9-18).

With Moses gone 40 days, the people's faith failed. They asked Aaron to make them gods. Aaron gathered their gold jewelry, and molded them into a golden calf. Then said, *"These are your gods, O Israel, who brought you up out of Egypt."* They bowed down and sacrificed to it (Ex. 32:1-6).

God was furious! How Moses talked with God while He was this angry with the people is important and provides many lessons. Moses' confronting God's anger is in Exodus 32.

When the people worshiped the golden calf, the Lord was so angry He considered destroying them. He called them corrupt and stiff-necked. For years, they had prayed to be saved from slavery, and now that the Lord had answered, they rejected Him in favor of an idol. We act in similar ways. We seek His help and then credit ourselves (self-worship) for achieving any good outcome. We surely hurt Him as deeply.

God ordered Moses to return to the people. He asked to be alone so His anger could burn against them that He might destroy them. Still, He told Moses, *"I will make you into a great nation"* (Ex. 32:10). Note: while angry enough to destroy the people, He ensured Moses knew he would be saved and blessed as a great nation. God always rewards faithfulness.

Moses, who began with the Lord by saying he was slow of speech, was now prepared to stand up to the Lord and plead for the people. After the Egyptian plagues, Moses knew God was capable of destroying them, and He had a good reason. Still, he also knew that God loved them enough to save them from slavery. If this was going to test his loyalty, Moses would pass. Moses had been told to lead the people, and he would defend them so he could. Moses would put his faith to the challenge.

While Moses had been afraid of God when he met Him at the burning bush, he was no longer that spiritually immature, young man. The early Moses would likely have fled down the mountain, yelling at the people all the way. But because Moses now had a solid relationship with the Lord, he didn't fear pleading with Him. Even with the Lord being furious, Moses sought the favor of the LORD on the people's behalf (v.11).

At first, God distanced Himself from the sinful people, and called them Moses' people: *Go down, because **your people, whom you brought** up out of Egypt have become corrupt* (v.7). God saw nothing spiritual in them. They were too worldly to belong to Him. It appeared Moses needed to remember whose people they were and not become so identified with them that he thought he was accountable for their actions. God needed Moses to know he would still lead them after their horrible sin, because they would turn away multiple times to worship idols. Moses needed to accept they were God's responsibility, not his, and realize he would not use such sin as an excuse to abandon them.

Moses could not argue that the people were worth saving, but he did remember God loved them. Moses proved his faithfulness by refusing to let the Lord tell him they were his people. He boldly turned God's words around: *"Why should Your anger burn against* **Your people, whom You brought** *out of Egypt with great power and a might hand?"* Moses reminded that although they had sinned greatly, they were still the Lord's chosen ones. Moses was saving them from Egypt's slavery, not because of anything he had done, but because God loved them enough to free them. Regardless of how sinful another becomes, God still loves the person, and by remembering that, we can always pray for others, no matter how horrible their sins.

Moses reminded the Lord: *"Why should the Egyptians say, 'It was with evil intent that He brought them out, to kill them in the mountains and to wipe them off the face of the earth?' Turn from your fierce anger: relent and do not bring disaster on your people"* (Ex. 32:12). Being forced to defend the people, Moses became more committed to them.

His many prayers are surely what made Moses a man of God and one to whom the Lord would welcome an argument. Moses' desire for the people to do what's right made him the correct choice to lead them. Caring that our children do right in the Lord's sight is what makes a parent good in God's eyes. It's what makes a supervisor seem good to his subordinates. And talking often with the Lord makes us a Moses-type person.

Moses needed reassurance that God would still save the people. So, he continued asking God to change His mind, if for no other reason, because of His prior promises to godly men: *"Remember your servants, Abraham, Isaac, and Israel, to whom you swore by your own self: 'I will make your descendants as numerous as the stars in the sky, and I will give your descendants all this land I promised them., and it will be their inheritance forever"* (Ex. 32:13). God needed Moses to know that He keeps His promises, even when people don't.

Moses knew how deeply the Lord loved the sinful people and wanted to give them a land flowing with milk and honey. God wanted them to repent and stay loyal, not be destroyed. After Moses recalled God's prior promises, the Lord relented and did not bring His threatened disaster (v. 14). However, that should not be taken as His no longer being furious with their idolatrous worship.

Moses had passed God's test and proven his loyalty to the people and to God. God was convinced Moses would plead with the people to turn back to Him, no matter how often they disobeyed. God has always required the same of men.

For example, God commanded Ezekiel (33:7-9) to warn the people of their sinfulness and persuade them to change. If Ezekiel didn't try, God said he too would be lost. We are told in Galatians (6:1) that we are to help restore one caught in sin. God doesn't want to lose a one of His children and expects us to be His earthly messengers to help save the lost.

God doesn't want to lose a one of His children and expects us to be His earthly messengers to help save the lost

Moses could have sided with the Lord and told Him to destroy the people. But being a man of faith, he could not do that. Although Moses was furious with their sin, he pleaded for the corrupt transgressors. May we learn from Moses' story, that in the face of the most unthinkable sin of another, we should immediately pray to remove the sinner from Satan's grip. May we never see another's sin as too terrible or the person so corrupt that we fail to pray for the person's removal from their slavery of sin. Moses proved how love covers a multitude of sins (1 Pe. 4:8). With love, we want the sinner to change, not reject him.

Moses was equally angry with the people. When he left the mountain and found them partying, he furiously smashed the stones with the Ten Commandments. Moses agreed with the Lord: they were corrupt. Moses had traveled enough miles with them to know how immoral they could act. They grumbled and complained and blamed Moses for everything they disliked. This explains why God needed Moses to know he would press them to remain faithful no matter how often they blamed Moses for things they hated. Now, they had done what throughout history, God warned people not to do: created an idol and worshiped it. Moses knew God required death for such sin. He would prove faithful in serving God by administering their death penalty.

Moses knew that not all two million people had sinned and did not judge all by the sins of some. He asked for all who were for the Lord to come with him., and the Levites responded. They strapped a sword to their sides and walked among the camp, each killing his neighbor. Because they did as told, the Levites were set apart to serve the Lord as priests. Still, Moses prayed for the people because he knew God loved them. Likewise, God welcomes us arguing when our goal is to save another's soul.

God welcomes us arguing when our goal is to save another's soul

Moses told the people they had committed a great sin, and he would try to make atonement for them. When Moses met God, he admitted how horrible the people's sin was. Then he pleaded: *Please forgive their sin – but if not, then blot me out of the Book You have written"* (v.33). Moses was willing to place the security of his own soul beside those for whom he pleaded forgiveness. Moses was asking God to save them because of his faith. If God wouldn't do that, Moses said to kill him with them. This confirmed Moses loyalty to the people.

Paul said something similar: *I could wish that I myself were cursed and cut off from Christ for the sake of my brothers, those of my own race, the people of Israel* (Ro. 9:3). To be willing to spend eternity in hell if it would save another's soul is the most loyal, genuine love.

As a mother, I understand. It's a love every mother feels for her unfaithful children. She cannot bear the thought of them burning in hell for eternity. She would die to save them if there was a way. Prayer is the way to pursue the Lord's help, because Jesus is the way, the truth, and life of salvation (Jn. 10:10). We need to remember that our children are helpless against our ceaseless prayers.

There are other lessons to learn from Moses' interaction with God. One is applying God's way if you have a child, say a daughter, who is dating a boy you think is a bad influence. Most parents want to point out all the boy's flaws and wrongs, failing to realize this tends to have her defending him. The more negative the parents say about the boy, the more she feels forced to protect him, and the stronger she is likely to bond with him. Instead, they need to draw the bad boy into the family gatherings and private times. They need to pray for him and with him, and find something neutrally nice to say to her about him. This either lets the parents realize they were mistaken about the boy, or it lets their daughter realize how embarrassed she is by how he acts around others. It forces her to see the negative qualities her parents see and has her deciding if she can tolerate such behavior. It's what let Moses destroy those who sinned (he saw their wrongs and could not deny them) but still he pled for those who had not sinned (having defended them, he bonded with those who did no wrong). Defending another helps you bond with him, but being forced to see them do wrong again and again, breaks the emotional tie.

The **Lord blotted out of His Book all those who sinned** that day, and struck them with a plague (Ex. 32:15-35). This story shows how seriously the Lord considers sin, and it reveals that a record of people's behaviors is kept in a Book in heaven, unless we give God reason to blot us out.

God told Moses to lead the people and an angel would go before him, (Ex. 33:3). The people were distressed, as we all should be when we sin and anger the Lord by putting our idols before Him. It's also a lesson that shows the faster we humbly confess our sin, the quicker God's anger cools.

GOD'S JEALOUS FOR US

Moses met with the Lord in a tent outside the camp. *The LORD would speak to Moses face to face, as a man speaks with his friend* (Ex. 33:11). After the people's great sin, Moses was concerned who would help him lead them. He asked God, *"If you are pleased with me, teach me your ways so I may know You and continue to find favor with You. Remember that this nation is Your people"* (v. 13). The LORD promised to go with him and give him rest.

Still, Moses wanted more assurance and pleaded if God's presence wasn't going with them, then do not send them. He asked, *"How will anyone know You are pleased with me and with Your people unless You go with us? What else will distinguish me and Your people from all other people on the face of the earth"* (v. 16)?

Scripture says God agreed to do as Moses asked because He was pleased with Moses and knew him by name. The Lord's agreement gave Moses the courage to ask, *"Now show me your glory"* (v.18).

The LORD responded, *"I will cause all my goodness to pass in front of you, and I will proclaim My name, the LORD, in your presence.* Moses chiseled two stone tablets like the first ones that had contained the Ten Commandments, so God would write the same words again. When Moses retuned to Mount Sinai, the Lord was prepared to show Moses His glory. The Lord hid Moses in the cleft of a rock, covered him with His hand, and allowed Moses to see His back because no one could see His face and live.

As the Lord passed by Moses, He emphasized His name twice: the LORD, the LORD. Then, He described Himself as: compassionate, gracious, slow to anger, abounding in love, abounding in faithfulness, maintaining love to thousands, and forgiving wickedness, rebellion, and sin. His glory revealed His perfect holiness. His flawless character. His holy goodness. And the Lord reminded Moses that He does not leave the guilty unpunished. His holiness will not let Him do otherwise. Moses immediately bowed to the ground and worshiped, asking the Lord to forgive their wickedness (Ex. 34:1-9).

After being this close to the glory of the Lord, Moses' face radiated so strongly, he scared the people. He wore a veil over his face and removed it only when talking with the Lord.

Throughout history, God has shown His glorious holiness to men, and the glory has always scared them and had them trembling in fear. But afterwards, they often did something for the Lord. Recall at the burning bush that Moses was afraid to look, and yet, think about all he did for the Lord. Isaiah (6:3) heard angels call out, *"Holy, holy, holy is the Lord almighty; The whole earth is filled with His glory and he (Isaiah) was afraid.* Afterwards, Isaiah carried God's message to the people. David said the heavens declare the glory of God and the skies the work of His hand (Ps. 19:1). Habakkuk's heart pounded and lips quivered, as he described God's holiness as sun rays flashing from His hand (3:3-16). Ezekiel saw the Lord's glory and immediately fell to the ground before being told to eat a sweet tasting scroll, containing words he was to tell the people (Eze. 1:1-28). The glory of the Lord shone round the shepherds as the angels announced the birth of Jesus. The men were terrified (Lk. 2:9), and afterwards, they went to search for Him. When Jesus took Peter, James, and John with Him up the mountain to pray, Jesus was transfigured before them. His face shone like the sun, and His clothes became as white as light. The disciples were scared and fell face down to the ground (Mt. 17:1-8; Mk. 9:2-8; Lk 9: 9 Jn. 28-36). They understood that Jesus had been describing John. In heaven, we will no longer need the sun or moon because the Lord's glory - His holy qualities - will be our light (Rev. 21:23). In every example, glory represented a light purer and brighter than what men had seen before. The Father's glory is so powerful and majestic that even heaven's seraphs' cover their faces and do not look directly at Him (Isa. 6:2). His glory reveals His goodness and His love for mankind, so much so, He is jealous when men do wrong and choose to follow Satan over Him. He knows the end result if we don't put Him first so we can spend eternity in heaven with Him. He doesn't want us in hell because we choose Satan.

Why did the holy brightness of God's glory cause all men to feel terrified, even the men closest to Jesus? Isaiah (6:1-8) explains. Isaiah saw the Lord seated on a throne, and His robe filled the temple, as seraph called out God's holiness. When the doorposts shook and smoke filled the temple, Isaiah was horrified. Fearing he was going to die, Isaiah knew *"I am a man of unclean lips."* Being close to the Lord's holiness, he could not deny his own sinfulness. How dreadfully dirty sin must appear against God's holy brilliance.

Is there anyone today who has clean lips? Who hasn't spoken a sinful word? While standing face-to-face with the Lord's untainted, pure goodness, our sin cannot be hidden or denied. Our miniscule amount of goodness will reveal our utter failure when contrasted with Jesus' glorious holiness. It will let us understand why He is jealous when we choose to do wrong.

Our miniscule amount of goodness will reveal our utter failure when contrasted with Jesus' holiness

The Lord had told Moses He was making a Covenant to do wonders never before done in any nation, and the people living around them would see the awesomeness of His work. God wasn't after praise. He wanted men to realize His power and love for them. He wanted them to know He would care for them so more people would want to join His eternal heavenly family. God wanted the Israelites to drive out the many wicked clans who worshiped idols, not make a treaty with them. They used young children as part of their sacrifices to Molech and Baal (Lev 20:2-5; Dt. 12:31), which God sternly condemned.

God not only required the death of parents who sacrificed their child to an idol, but He condemned anyone who failed to kill these parents. He told Moses: *"Any Israelite or any alien living in Israel who gives any of his children to Molech must be put to death. The people of the community are to stone him. I will set my face against that man, and I will cut him off from his people; for by giving his children to Molech, he has defiled my sanctuary and profaned My holy name. If the people of the community close their eyes when that man gives one of his children to Molech, and they fail to put him to death, I will set my face against that man and his family and will cut off from their people both him and all who follow him in prostituting themselves to Molech"* (Lev. 20:2-5; Dt. 12:31; 18:18). How angry God must be when we parents place our kids' education or careers before Him, and they sacrifice having a relationship with Him in order to succeed in their worldly idols.

God takes it equally as serious when we put our own idols of careers, our spouse/children, recreation, or whatever before our relationship with Him. He said, *"Do not worship any other god, for the LORD, whose name is Jealous, is a jealous God"* (Ex. 20:5). Jesus is a jealous God because of how deeply He loves

His followers. What a blessing to be this loved by a Holy God who is jealous when we do things on our own without seeking His guidance or when we listen to Satan. He knows how this always creates difficulties for us that could have been avoided. He wants us to continually recall the many times He has already blessed us, because when we do, it reassures us that He will continue doing so in the future. He wants to give us only love, and cares if we commit spiritual adultery that requires Him to punish us.

He is jealous because no matter how good we try to be, our own goodness won't save us (2 Tim. 1:9). Only Jesus' righteousness saves. None are good enough, nor do enough good deeds to deserve heaven. He jealously wants to help us do our best to image Him and wishes all would want to be saved. It is why He came to seek and save the lost (Lk. 19:10). He wants everyone to come to repentance (2 Pe. 3:9).

When the Israelites finally reached the Jordan, they were too fearful of the huge people on the other side of the river to cross over and take the Promised Land flowing with milk and honey. They ignored that God had promised an angel would defeat their enemies. Because of this, God refused to let them cross until all of the people over age 20 had died, and He renewed His Covenant with them.

This version of the Covenant obligated everyone: leaders, chief men, elders, officials, other men, their wives, and aliens living in their camp (Dt. 29:10-11). This group included all nations through whom every person today has come. We know that everyone came from Adam (Ac.17:26) and Eve (Ge. 3:20, then through Noah. God said, *"I am making this Covenant, with its oath, not only with you who are standing here with us today in the presence of the Lord our God, but **also with those who are not here today"** (Dt. 29:15 my emphasis). This Covenant included those who lived in the past, those present that day, and those who would live in the future, including us.

God's plan was always for Him to have a close, bonded family-type relationship with everyone while they lived on earth and then forever together in heaven. Since Adam, He has wanted to give men blessings, and only used punishment for disobedience in hope that their fearing His retribution would have them obey.

The Mosaic Law was meant to continue revealing God's holy character to future generations. It included them being careful to live according to the words of the law. It was for their children, who had not known it, to hear and learn to fear the Lord, as long as they lived in the land they were going over the Jordan to possess (Dt. 31:12-13). The law taught what qualified as sin and wrongdoing. Paul says it is because of the law that we know what sin is (Ro. 3:20).

The foundation of the renewed Covenant was grace, just as the Lord forgave the people's sins each year when they sacrificed the blood of a perfect animal. Having these blood reminders helped them understand their need for a perfect Savior who would one day sacrifice His own blood to remove the sins of all in the world (Jn. 1:29).

Still, the people of Israel repeatedly broke their Covenant promise and were eventually sent into exile. For the Lord GOD said, *"I will deal with you as you deserve, because you have despised My oath by breaking the Covenant."* (Eze. 16:59 my emphasis). We make a similar oath when we are baptized (1 Pe. 3:21), and God warns us of breaking our pledge. God hates and punishes sin. Yet, He is merciful and forgiving when man repents. God is holy and deserves man's worship because of His goodness to which man's good qualities and actions cannot compare.

The Lord GOD said, "I will deal with you as you deserve, because you have despised My oath by breaking the Covenant"

The Lord used both love and fear to motivate the Israelites not to sin and to increase their faith. *To fear the Lord is to hate sin* (Prov. 8:13), and *great is His love for those who fear Him*

(Prov.1:7). Deuteronomy (5:29) describes how God loved the Israelites and how He loves us today: *Oh, that their hearts would be inclined to fear me and keep all my commands always, so that it might go well with them and their children forever!* God has always wanted what's best for His creations and is jealous when they stray because He knows the problems that come with disobedience. He is jealous because He wants to love us throughout all of eternity and knows He must punish our disobedience if we follow Satan instead.

Moses saw the Promised Land but he did not get to step foot on it. Earlier, he had disobeyed and struck the rock to have it flow with water for the thirsty, complaining people. *God split the rocks in the desert and gave them water as abundant as the seas* (Ps. 78:15). Moses took God's glory by letting the people credit him for their having water, instead of praising and thanking God. He was punished for **his sin of taking God's glory for himself** (Dt. 32:51 my emphasis). God wanted the people to realize it was Him who cared for them so they would be faithful and learn to love Him.

Although taking God's glory was sinful, Moses was called God's friend, as Abraham had been. Such a blessing to have that close a relationship with the Lord.

Moses' relationship with the Lord was so special, he even had God defend him. When Miriam and Aaron disapproved of a woman Moses married, Jesus met them in a pillar of cloud at the entrance to the Tent of Meeting to explain how He felt about Moses: *"He is faithful in all my house.* **With him I speak face to face***, clearly and not in riddles;* **he sees the form of the Lord***. Why then were you not afraid to speak against my servant, Moses?"* Jesus described Moses as being humbler than anyone else on the face of the earth (Nu. 12:3). Imagine having Jesus defend you to others – and yet we know, He defends us to His Father each time we repent, and on Judgment Day, He will defend the faithful (Ro. 8:34; 1 Tim. 2:5).

How was Moses able to cling so tightly to Jesus? Moses continually kept his thoughts and decisions on eternity. In his earlier years, he had chosen eternity with the Lord over all the wealth that was his as the son of Pharaoh's daughter. How might we change if we did the same and asked ourselves, *"Will spending this money or doing this activity help me go to heaven or to hell?"* Or if we questioned, *"Will my doing this bring me closer to the Lord or closer to Satan?"* Remember Jesus said you are either with me or against me. He has no middle ground. Once Moses made the commitment to spend eternity with the Lord, this goal determined his every decision. He knew what he wanted and spent his life focused on living eternally in heaven.

Once we make the same commitment, heaven belongs to us, and a place reserved in heaven is already ours.

CHANGING DAVID'S HEART

Throughout the Old Testament, the Israelites were repeatedly told that they did not deserve the Promised Land and its wealth. Moses cautioned Israel that they were not to claim that God drove out the pagans because Israel was righteous, but they were required to acknowledge God did so because the pagan nations were so wicked (Dt. 9:4-6; Eze. 36:22). Yet, because of the Lord's faithfulness to the Covenant promises made to their forefathers, He gave the Israelites the land and fulfilled His commitment with Abraham, Isaac, and Jacob. When God makes a promise, nothing men can do will change His plan.

After taking Canaan, the Israelites again practiced idolatry, and were subdued by their enemies. As their conditions worsened, they called on God for help. He gave them Judges who kept them in fear of Him until each Judge died. This cycle repeated multiple times as the civil law and religion struggled to remain compatible. What set Israel apart was that their nation was the special possession of the one true God (Dt. 7:6). They belonged to Him, so He kept taking them back for the same loving reason He welcomes home repentant, straying Christians today. God loves those who are His own, no matter their actions, just as parents with rebellious children do.

When God's priests became evil, the people hated the required animal sacrifices. Once the Ark that held the Covenant, the symbol of God's presence, was stolen by the Philistines, the people begged to have a king to lead them. Only they didn't want one to help them be closer to God. They wanted a king to be like their neighbors, and God let them have Saul.

In his paranoia, Saul slaughtered the priests who tended the tabernacle at Nob. He no longer sought the Lord because Abiathar, the remaining priest, took the ephod with him when he fled (1 Sam. 22; 23). The worship of the Lord was so diminished that Saul sought guidance from the witch of Endor, a spiritualist medium, and the Lord condemns seeking advice from such sources (1 Sam. 28). Saul won many battles, but his selfishness turned him away from God, and he eventually died on a battlefield. During their time of having kings, God told the people, "**You <u>despised</u> *My oath*** by breaking the Covenant and following worthless idols and doing things forbidden to do (Eze. 16:59; 2 Ki. 17:15 my emphasis).

God told the people, "You <u>despised</u> *My oath* by breaking the Covenant and following worthless idols

After Saul, God chose David, the young shepherd boy who had killed the giant, Goliath, and credited the Lord for his victory. His becoming king fulfilled an earlier promise to Abraham and Sarah that their offspring would include kings. The early part of King David's reign was one of faithfulness to the Lord. God's Covenant with David pointed to both Solomon, David's son, and to Jesus, Son of God the Father.

The Covenant with David was an unconditional Covenant. Its fulfillment did not depend on David's behavior, and it was a good thing, because both David and his son, Solomon, committed grievous sins that hurt God deeply (2 Sam. 11:1-27; 1 Ki. 11:4-9). But God had purposed to keep His promise, and He would fulfill it regardless of their actions (2 Tim. 2:13). God's Covenant promise was to establish David's house through Solomon. David's throne would be eternal because it was a prophecy of the coming of our Messiah, Jesus (Mt. 21:9). God's promise was to make David's name greatest of all men on earth. God said He would punish his son, Solomon, when he did wrong, but he would love him forever, and his house and kingdom would be forever established with a man sitting on the throne, meaning Jesus Christ, our King (2 Sam. 7:12-16; 1 Ch. 17:11-15; 1 Ki. 8:25; Jer. 33:14-17; Ps. 132:11).

For the people to receive His blessings, their part of the Covenant was conditional and contingent upon Israel's adherence to the Law. God promised to bless them with a home of their own where they would no longer be disturbed by their enemies. The blessings and curses that are associated with this part of the Covenant are detailed in Deuteronomy 28.

The seriousness of the Covenant with David was backed by God's faithfulness, as given in Psalm (89:34-36): *I will not take My love from him nor will I ever betray My faithfulness. I will not violate My Covenant or alter what My lips have uttered. Once for all, I have sworn My holiness – and I will not lie to David – his line will continue forever.* Through Jesus Christ it continues today and until Jesus returns.

However, when most people hear the name of King David, they remember his sin with Bathsheba, not the good he did. He has been dead for centuries, and yet, his sin is still what most remember. We need to realize it's our sinful wrongs that are remembered about us too, but once forgiven by the Lord, we know other's memories do not matter, just as it no longer did with David. Because when we are right with God, people's judgments have no bearing on our eternity.

Whether David used his power as king to rape Bathsheba or if she chose to bathe when he would be atop his roof in hope of seducing him is not what's most important. Nor is it that David had her husband, Uriah, killed after David learned she was pregnant with his child. The significance that is too often overlooked is what God said that changed David's heart, and how it had him seeking forgiveness and promising faithfulness to the Lord.

After David's sexual relationship with Bathsheba, God sent Nathan to tell David a story that had David realizing he was the central player in the story who had sinned. What God had Nathan say next transformed David, spiritually and emotionally. *"I anointed you king over Israel, and I delivered you from the hand of Saul. I gave your master's house to you, and your master's wives into your arms. I gave you the house of Israel and Judah. And if all this had been too little, I would have given you even more. Why did* **you despise the word of the Lord by doing what is evil** *in His eyes? You struck down Uriah the Hittite with the sword and took his wife to be your own. You killed him with the sword of the Ammonites. Now, therefore the sword will never depart from your house because* **you despised Me** *and took the wife of the Hittite to be your own."* (2 Sam. 12:8-10 my emphasis).

Why did you <u>despise</u> <u>the word</u> of the Lord and <u>despise</u> <u>the Lord</u> by doing what is evil?

How much stronger could Jesus emphasize that to sin is to hate His word and despise Him? Note that adultery was described as a sin against God's Word, and killing one who had converted to follow the Lord was a sin against God. David didn't attempt to rationalize his actions, deny them, or excuse them. Instead, he hung his head and cried, *"I have sinned against You."*

When I realized the seriousness of what this implied for me today, unlike David, I wanted to argue. I kept thinking, *"No, I love you, Jesus. I just don't think and do wrong sometimes."* But He stopped my defense. I felt crushed once I admitted He was right. I sat crying for quite a while, remembering a long list of sins I had committed and pleaded with God to forgive each wrong. Many sins, I had previously repented of and knew God didn't remember them, but I realized my lack of doing right meant I didn't have enough of His Word or love for Him in my heart. My lack of knowledge of His Word and love for Him was what I repented this time. Had I known enough and loved Him enough, my faith would have stopped me. I confessed having too little faith. God saying *'when you sin, you despise My Word and Me'* reminded that I wasn't praying often enough and was trying to handle things on my own, just as men from Adam to David had done.

Now, I could genuinely understand their sin of doing things their way, instead of first seeking the Lord's guidance. What great applicable lessons are found in the lives of the Old

Testament people. No wonder, Paul said these things were written down as warnings for us, and no temptation has seized you except what is common to man (1 Cor. 10: 11,13). Healthy spiritual and emotional living comes by embracing how God tell us to deal with sin and that's with ongoing confessions and change, just as David did.

David's adultery had led him to commit multiple sins. For example, God's people were not to marry Hittites. However, Uriah, a Hittite, had obviously converted to worship the Lord, or he wouldn't have been serving in David's army. So, David having Uriah killed when he had converted to serve the Lord was another sin. Imagine what David's having him killed taught other Hittite's who might have been considering converting to worship the one true Lord. Nathan told David, *"You have made the enemies of the Lord show utter contempt" (v. 14).* Or as Paul later said, "You suppress truth by your wickedness (Ro. 1:18).

David later asked: *May those who hope in you not be disgraced because of me. . . may those who seek you not be put to shame because of me* (Ps. 69:6). David realized how the depth of his sin had negatively impacted on others.

For Uriah to be killed by an Ammonite's sword was another bad mark against David. By the Ammonites killing Uriah, they had successfully murdered another who worshiped the true Lord. The Ammonites were an evil group, and God wanted all of them destroyed so the Israelites wouldn't be tempted to participate in their wicked practices. Their killing Uriah brought success and praise for their clan and their false god, while if Uriah had lived, he could have given God glory by helping to destroy the evil ones. David's sexual sin had been the first of many sins as he attempted to conceal his adultery.

During my years of doing counseling, I found that sexual sin is among the early sins committed by people who stray from the Lord. Once they stop praying and reading God's Word, they feel empty, lonely, unloved, and estranged from others. Their loneliness, lets Satan tempt them with a longing for sexual closeness with another. They falsely think it will satisfy their emptiness. Instead of it working, they have added another sin to their tall stack, and then another sin, as they lie to hide it, and another as they waste money to support the sinful relationship. Satan never stops with man committing just one sin. Satan wants the whole package. *He prowls around like a roaring lion looking for someone to devour* (1 Peter 5:8). Destroying one spiritually is Satan's goal because he knows how it pains God.

According to the Law, both David and Bathsheba should have been killed for their adultery, but God let them live.

However, God warned that their son would die, and David should expect tragedy among his family. David's other children became unruly rebels who committed wrongs against each other and against David. David was seen as a kind, forgiving man of other's wrongs, but he was severely lacking as a father. But God telling him that to sin is to hate God grabbed his attention, and it was obviously something he never forgot.

Once David recognized how the Lord viewed his sin, he spent days fasting, lying on the floor, and praying. David sought forgiveness for his sins. *"Against You, You only, have I sinned and done what is evil in Your sight, so that You are proved right when You speak and justified when You judge (Ps.51:4).* He pleaded for God to forgive him and cleanse his heart. David acknowledged knowing what God wanted was a broken spirit and a contrite heart. And David's humble, honest admission of wrong offered the Lord just that.

Once David was told of his newborn son's death, he cleaned himself, worshiped, and ate. He admitted knowing he was forgiven by the Lord, and one day, **would again see his infant son in heaven** (2 Sam. 22-23 my emphasis). What a special promise for parents who lose a child, one of the most painful of loses.

It's interesting that David cleansed himself of sin before worshipping the Lord. Today, we are told that taking communion is to remind us of the high cost of God's forgiveness (1 Peter 1:18–19). Partaking of the bread and wine vividly depicts our union with Christ as our Lord, Savior, and Source of spiritual life (Jn. 14:6, 5:21; Ps. 36:9). Like David, we fall short, and sin in ways that deserve death. Our task is to frequently repent, so we are forgiven, and are cleaner as we worship the Lord. *Only fools mock at making amends for their sins* (Prov. 14:9).

David's strength was his willingness to overlook others' sins, while being unwilling to ignore his own. Twice, he had opportunity to kill Saul but he spared him (1 Sam. 24:3-7; 26:2-12). Saul opposed David continually, but when Saul died, David wept for him and for his son Jonathan (2 Sam.1:11-12). David was especially kind and good to the crippled orphan, Mephibosheth (2 Sam. 9:1-13). David didn't hold grudges or try to get even for any mistreatment. He loved his enemies, and welcomed back rebels. He overlooked the sins of his opposition. He knew how to forgive, but he also knew how to genuinely repent of his own wrongs. He knew his God was the one true God and that other gods were just idols made by humans (Ps. 115:3-7,135:13-17). David led his people with integrity of heart and skillful hands (Ps. 78:71).

The only person David was stern with was himself. He was honest about all his mistakes and confessed them. He understood that each sin was first and foremost a sin against God, and he was determined to live forgiven. David's enthusiasm for serving God, affected the entire nation. After retrieving the Ark of the Covenant from his enemies, He was so excited that he danced for joy in the streets (2 Sam. 6:14). After his sin with Bathsheba, David endeavored to be used for and by God and remain God's spiritual servant.

He was a man after God's own heart because he hated his own sins, but he worked to forgive others. How like the Lord, King David was in forgiveness. God welcomes his enemies to come home, repent, and have every sin forgiven and forgotten—permanently (Heb. 8:12). Jesus died in sinners' place to ensure them a home as family of the heavenly Godhead. How David must have loved knowing that through his genealogy our Savior, Jesus Christ, would come.

Although David wanted to build God a temple, God would not let him. His son, Solomon, built it, using a large amount of pure gold that David donated (1. Chron. 29:1-4).

The Lord offered to let Solomon make one request, and Solomon pleased Him by asking for wisdom. Solomon gained the reputation of being the wisest man ever to live. But like many before him, Solomon married women who led him astray to worship false gods. He married 700 unbelieving wives from the very clans God had condemned and who sacrificed children to idols. Solomon even built an altar for their worship (1 Ki.11:1-8).

Solomon indulged in every type of worldly luxury. He tried everything, but when he left out God, nothing satisfied his hunger for real meaning and secure love. (Ecc. 12: 1-8). How sad that it takes many of us so many wasted years to learn we need God to feel complete by knowing we can have the blessed assurance of eternal salvation. As Solomon faced death, he understood that all human efforts apart from God are meaningless.

After Solomon's death, the kingdom declined with weak leaders and the breaking away of ten Israelite tribes that intermingled with pagan groups. The sins of the kings of Judah and Israel were so major that Israel was expelled from the land. God removed the very ones through whom His Covenant promises were to come. Thankfully, the promise made in Genesis 3:15, as God cursed the serpent, was unconditional. Regardless of people's sins, our Savior would still come

For many years, the Israelites were scattered and enslaved. They hoped for the coming of the prophesied Messiah spoken about by Isaiah (11:1). *"A shoot will come up from the stump of Jesse, from the roots, a Branch will bear fruit. The Spirit of the Lord will rest on Him - the Spirit of wisdom and of understanding, the Spirit of counsel and of power, the Spirit of knowledge and of the fear of the Lord- and He will delight in the fear of the Lord.* Jeremiah foretold of the coming of a new law that would be written on the hearts of men (31:31-34). Other prophets foretold of a new Covenant, a Savior, His Church, and the Holy Spirit.

However, there remained a major concern. The Gentiles were missing. The promise conceived in heaven was to include all mankind, not just the Israelites and the aliens who had joined them. Paul explained that the Gentiles were included in God's salvation plan to make Israel envious and to bring the Israelites back to the Lord. It was Israel's rejection of the Lord's commands that helped reconcile all people in the world (Ro. 11:11-23). Because the Israelites had intermarried so often with the Gentiles, the only way to bring the Israelites back to the Lord was to also save the Gentiles. God made the two become one in Him and destroyed the dividing wall of hostility (Eph. 2:14). *His purpose was to create in Himself one new man out of the two, thus making peace, and in this one body to reconcile both of them to God through the cross* (v. 15).

Gentiles were included in God's salvation plan to make Israel envious and to bring the Israelites back to the Lord.

Early examples of Gentiles being saved are the Roman centurion (Mt. 8), Canaanite woman (Mt. 15); Cornelius (Ac 10), and others. Paul called the Israelites a wild branch that had broken off because of unbelief. However, he assured that with faith, they could be grafted in.

The Law of Moses told the people of Israel what they should and should not do, but it was incapable of supplying them with a heart that desired to obey. Many who were circumcised in his flesh were not circumcised in their hearts, and physical circumcision was abandoned by some. The Law had no power to give people a new heart, and the people were unable to obey the Law perfectly (Gal. 3:21). Many people memorized the Law, but that didn't give them the will to obey what the Law said.

Jeremiah (24:7) fore told that God was going to give them a better heart. *"I will give them a heart to know me, that I am the Lord. They will be My people and I will be their God for they will return to Me with all their heart."*

For generations, the Father had reached out to men to prepare them for the day His holy Son would sacrifice for their sins of continued disobedience. However, by the time Jesus was born, the Jews were awaiting the arrival of a great military leader. The people's concern was their cruel treatment by the Romans, and they thought this new leader would free them from Roman rule, as Moses had freed their ancestors from Egyptian rule. Their misunderstanding of what God had planned led to their rejection and crucifixion of Jesus Christ, the one for whom they had waited so long.

From Genesis chapter one and onward, we find stories of God's love for His creation, the people having doubts, falling prey to sinful temptations, and always wanting to return to Him and receive the blessings found in His Covenants. The Law was put in place to let them see how sinful they were and recognize their need for a Savior so they might be justified by faith and receive God's grace (Gal. 3:24).

The importance of David's lineage was acknowledged when the angel Gabriel appeared to Mary in Luke (1:31–33) my emphasis). He told her, *"Behold, you will conceive in your womb and bear a Son and you shall call His name Jesus. He will be great and will be called the Son of the Most High; and the Lord God will give to Him the* **throne of his father David,** *and He will reign over the house of Jacob forever, and* **of His kingdom there will be no end.**" Jesus called Himself the Root and Offspring of David (Rev. 22:16). The promises given in all prior Covenants were to be fulfilled by Jesus Christ.

We have the choice to be a part of God's kingdom that has no end. We can live as David did, repenting often of our sins so we live knowing we are part of the Godhead's heavenly family. Jesus died so a perfect God – man relationship would last forever. His part is complete. It's now our decision.

NEW COVENANT

Old Testament people had promises; people under the New Covenant have fulfillment of the promises (Heb. 8-9). The gospel of Matthew opens by calling Jesus Christ the Son of David and the Son of Abraham (Matt. 1:1), with His right to rule over God's people. As the Son of David (Ro. 1:3), and also the Lord of David (Mt. 22:45; Ps. 110:1), Jesus reigns as king and high priest in heaven (1 Cor.15:25). He fulfilled the promises made with prior Covenants.

The New Covenant offers the way for one to be brought into the Godhead's family, and the way, truth, and life is through Jesus Christ. Since the time of Adam and Eve, the Father required men to pay for their sins with blood, but instead of requiring the blood of the guilt sinners, He allowed their use of another's blood. In Old Testament times, the priest carried out this responsibility. Only he used animal blood that was ineffective because animals' blood could not remove man's sin. (Heb. 10:4-6). Only blood of a perfect man would be an acceptable exchange to appease the Father's wrath of man's continued sins. And Jesus Christ was that perfect man.

Jesus flawlessly fulfilled the Old Covenant laws on our behalf (Mt. 5:18). Jesus died in our place to save us, by taking on Himself the Covenant curse's punishment that we deserve. When He cried, "My God, My God, why have you forsaken Me (Mt. 27:46-47; Mk. 15:34; Ps. 22:1), Jesus knew for a first time what it was like to be without His Holy Father. Jesus had the sins of every man and woman poured upon Him. Because the Father cannot be with sin, and Christ was covered with the sins of every person, Christ was abandoned by His Father. God expressed His pain of watching His Son in such agony with the sky turning black and the earth shacking. Never before had Jesus been totally separated from His Father, but now Jesus understood how painful it will be for people who reject Him and spend eternity in hell completely deserted by the Father. How they will miss all the good ways God daily cares for mankind.

Christ redeemed us from the Covenant curse by becoming a curse for us by dying on a tree. For it is written *"cursed is everyone who is hung on a tree"* (Gal. 3:13). When Christ died, the blessings given to Abraham were made available for Gentiles through Christ Jesus, and by faith they could now receive the Covenant's promises (v.14).

Jesus Christ bore all of mankind's sins in His own body (1 Pe. 2:24). He who knew no sin, became sin for us (2 Cor. 5:21). Jesus took the New Covenant curse so we believers don't have to know such anguish (Gal 3:13). Although He knew that He would be reunited with the Father, the agony of being separated from the Father for even a limited time caused Jesus deep cries of despair and suffering.

Jesus Christ's sacrificial blood made us right with the Father. In His role of Mediator, Jesus Christ brought the offer of peace between mankind and God (1Tim.2:5). As Mediator, Jesus understood the needs and responsibilities of both parties, so He could represent both mankind and the Father.

In order for Him to accurately represent mankind as a Mediator, Jesus came to earth to live. Jesus said, *"Sacrifice and offering You did not desire, but a body You prepared for Me. I have come to do Your will, O God"* (Heb. 10:5-7).

To understand our weaknesses, Jesus had to confront temptations like we face. To do this, He was born of a human mother. *We do not have a high priest who is unable to sympathize with our weaknesses, but we have one who has been tempted in every way, just as we are – yet was without sin* (Heb. 4:15). He never gave into Satan's snares (Mt. 4:1-11). Jesus coming to live as a human man let Him share in our humanity, and represent all of mankind as we address the Father.

Jesus is also truly God (Phil. 2:6-11). As God, He brings divine justice and grace to bear on us as He serves as Mediator for the Father. His blood sacrifice on the cross was what people, who have faith in Him, needed for being reconciled with the Father. The sins of every person from Adam to the last person living when Jesus comes again fell on Jesus on the cross. He appeared once for **all** to do away with sin by the sacrifice of Himself, once to take away the sins of many people (Heb. 9:26-28). *He was pierced for our transgressions, He was crushed for out iniquities; the punishment that brought us peace (with the Father) was upon Him, and by His wounds we are healed* (Isa. 53:5). Every sin of every person was credited to Christ and His righteousness gifted to mankind.

Jesus Christ's blood sacrifice paid our sin debt in full without the Father having to abandon His promised curse's punishment for our sins. *There is one God and one Mediator between God and men, the man Christ Jesus, who gave Himself as a ransom for all men - the testimony given in its proper time* (1 Tim. 2:5). As mediator, Jesus Christ's blood brought us and the Father together. **Jesus' blood and man's faith sets men free from sins**, and men can receive the Covenant promise of eternity (Heb. 9;15; 12:24 my emphasis). **He reconciled a world of sinners with God** (Ro. 5:6-11 my emphasis). Jesus took the deserved punishment of every person who has ever lived and who will one day live. He accepted the Covenant's curse and gave us His righteousness and redemption (1 Cor. 1:30), so we can become part of the holy Godhead's family. It is now mankind's choice to accept or reject His offer.

Jesus fulfilled the Father's set purpose. As Peter preached on Pentecost: *He was handed over to you by God's set purpose and foreknowledge; and you, with the help of wicked men, put Him to death by nailing Him to the cross. But God raised Him from the dead. . . because it was impossible for death to keep its hold on Him* (Ac. 2:22-24). Jesus' sinless perfection allowed the Father to accept His blood offering in exchange for the debts we owe for our sins and offer us permanent forgiveness. Jesus paid in full the debt of all of mankind's sins (Heb. 9:15). As proof of the Father's acceptance of Jesus' sacrifice, the Father raised Jesus from the dead, freeing Him from the agony of death. His body did not see decay. The Father raised Jesus to life, and exalted Jesus to sit at His right hand. Jesus entered the true sanctuary in heaven **to appear for us in the Father's presence** (Heb. 9:24 my emphasis). He is able **to save completely** those who come to the Father through Him **because He always lives to intercede for us** (Heb. 7:25 my emphasis).

Jesus' sinless perfection allowed the Father to accept His blood in exchange for the debts we owe for our sins and offer us permanent forgiveness

God saved us from sin and set us apart as His holy people. We are to obey His law and express our gratitude for His redemption. It's called being sanctified. By Jesus' one sacrifice

He made perfect forever those who are being made holy (Heb. 10:14).

Because Jesus Christ died for you and died for me is why you and I do not have to spend eternity in hell like we deserve. Our love for Him doing this should motivate our obedience. In remembrance of what He has done for us, we meet together every Sunday to share the Lord's Supper that He instituted as He shared Passover with His disciples. Acts (20:7) shows by example that the day for us sharing the Lord's Supper is the first day (Sunday) of each week.

The Father made Jesus our priest forever by oath (Heb. 7:18-21), making Jesus our guarantee of a better Covenant (Heb. 7:22). Jesus' sacrifice perfects believers for eternal life. The New Covenant offers salvation by the Father's grace through faith in the work of Jesus Christ for all men everywhere. All the ways of the Lord are loving and faithful for those who keep the demands of the Covenant (Ps. 25:10). The Lord confides in those who fear him and makes his Covenant known to them (Ps. 25:14).

As our High Priest, Jesus opened the way for us to go directly to our Heavenly Father by breaking the barrier that had separated us from Him. From the cross, *Jesus cried out again with a loud voice, and yielded up His spirit. Then behold, the veil of the temple was torn in two from top to bottom* (Mt. 27:50-51).

146

This was the heavy curtain/veil that had served as a room divider in the temple where people met to worship. It separated the Holy Place from the Most Holy Place where only the priest could go once a year to meet with God. But with Jesus' death, the separation of man from the Father was ended. Mankind could now go directly into the Father's presence and commune with Him in prayer.

Under the New Covenant, our relationship with the Father has changed and is much better. The Father's focus has always been to relate intimately and personally with His people, dwell among them, and dwell in them. Now, He can do this with His Son, Jesus Christ, and the Holy Spirit (Eph. 3:17). We can even call our Father, Abba, meaning we can have a child-like personal closeness, as a child who can ask his daddy for anything and share every delight and concern with Him. Paul described our relationship as a bondservant with his master. It's like a servant who is free to leave, but because of how kind the master is, the servant stays and remains loyal to the master.

As with prior Covenants, to receive God's blessings, people were required to agree to God's terms, and we are also required to agree to the requirements of the New Covenant. We are to be baptized to prove our faith in Jesus' sacrifice for us. Baptism shows we vow to be faithful. When we are baptized, we are given the Holy Spirit to live in our hearts to help us remain faithful and become more like Christ, and Christ adds us to His church. Jesus' Church or kingdom were foretold in the Old Testament by Daniel (2:44). John told us the only way to enter was by being born again (3:3), and Luke assured us His church will never end (1:33). The church and kingdom are one and the same, as revealed in Matthew, where the Lord declares to Peter, "*I will build My church*" and then said, "*I will give unto thee the keys of the kingdom of heaven*" (16:18-19). Jesus called it "My church" and immediately described the Church as "the kingdom of heaven."

In His church, we are united with Jesus Christ and with like believers throughout the world. We belong to Jesus Christ and He belongs to us. *I am my beloved's and my beloved is mine* (SS. 6:3). We are united to the Lord as a wife relates with love to her husband.

Jesus Christ is the Head of the Church, which is His body (Eph.1:22-23). As Paul wrote to the Corinthian believers, "*now you are the body of Christ, and each of you is a part of it.*" (1 Cor. 12:27). The Church is called the Body of Christ because members of the Body of Christ are joined to Christ in salvation (Eph. 4:16), with Christ as the Head (Eph. 1: 22-23). Christ takes people with different talents and personalities and unites them as a single body to care for each other and reach the lost for Him (1 Cor. 12:4-31. Note that it is not Peter's, or Paul's, or John's church. Nor is it the Church at South Street or Main Street. It is the Main Street Church of Christ. The Church belongs exclusively to Christ, not a street or of a different person's teaching. Jesus adds us to His church when we are baptized. We cannot add ourselves. It should carry a name that honors Him as its head.

Church members wear His name as Christians and serve as the Lord's representative in this world. They are indwelt by the Holy Spirit of Christ (Ro. 8:9). Together the members form one body that shares a common bond regardless of one's background, race, gender, or role of ministry. Jesus prayed for our unity, and for us to care for each other (1 Cor. 12:25). Faithful members are secure in their salvation (Jn. 10:28-30). They share in Christ's inheritance (Ro. 8:17).

As my husband and I traveled, we had the opportunity to worship with fellow believers where no English was spoken, and we felt comfortably at home. We partook of the Lord's Supper, and although, we didn't understand a word of the prayers, we knew their significance. While we couldn't sing the songs, we could hum with several. Afterwards, the warm handshakes let us know we belonged together. If we had experienced a crisis, we knew we would have been helped because that's what fellow believers do, even without speaking the same language.

With our commitment as Christ's Church to be faithful, we are family. We have the Holy Spirit who helps us understand His Word, and remain obedient. We are part of the holy family that's awaiting our trip home – to our permanent home.

"REMEMBER ME"

Jesus asks believers to share the Lord's Supper in remembrance of what He's done to offer us salvation. This chapter provides an explanation of why and how the Passover focus changed from the Israelites leaving Egypt to Jesus Christ's sacrifice. Likely, you have seen a picture of Jesus and the Apostles sitting at a table eating a meal. This chapter helps explain its popularity and importance that evening had to Jesus.

On the first day of the Feast of Unleavened Bread, when it was customary to sacrifice the Passover lamb, Jesus' disciples asked Him, *"Where do you want us to go and make preparations for you to eat the Passover?"* Jesus told Peter and John to go into the city and follow a man they would meet who was carrying a jar of water. When the man went into a house, they were to ask the owner for the guest room where they could eat the Passover. The owner showed them an upper room that was furnished and ready. (Mk. 14:112-14; Lk. 22:7-13).

Years earlier, the Lord had instructed the Israelites to honor special celebrations, one being the Passover that began at twilight on the 14th day of the first month of the Jewish calendar. On the following day (15th) the Feast of Unleavened

Bread began (Lev. 23:5). On the first and seventh day they could do no work. They were to remember how the Lord passed over His people in Egypt, and they were spared by having lamb's blood on their door posts. The Israelites celebrated the Festival of Unleavened Bread for seven days and ate nothing with leavening in it to symbolize how hastily they had left Egypt (Du. 16: 3; Ex. 12:17-20; 2 Ch. 30:21). Nor was any yeast to be in their houses during these seven days. The entire week was called the Feast of Unleavened Bread. Information about the Passover and the meal is taken from the internet sites of Jewish Library, Set Apart People, and Jewish History.

Passover was observed in homes until Solomon built the temple. Then, Jerusalem became the location for Passover, until Romans destroyed the temple, and it was again held in homes. Historians speculate that thousands of people yearly made the journey to Jerusalem, and locals opened rooms of their homes to accommodate such a crowd. Thus, Jesus and the apostles would have used such a room.

Finding things exactly as Jesus had told them, Peter and John prepared the Passover meal (Mk. 14:112-14; Lk. 22:7-13). With the room furnished and ready, it saved Peter and John a lot of time and work because the house would have been cleaned of all unleavened foods.

Today, Jews who celebrate the Passover begin by removing all ingredients that cause foods to rise. This requires weeks of scrubbing the kitchen as they clean appliances, and shelves that had contact with leavened products. The night before the meal, another search is conducted to ensure no leavening had been overlooked. Any found is burned the following morning. For seven days, no leavened products of any kind are allowed (Ex. 12:15; 13:7). God compared sin to leaven because both 'puff up' and grow (1 Cor. 5:1-8). To celebrate Passover, a special meal filled with rituals is held. This meal is called a Seder, meaning to observe the meal correctly, things must be done in a specific order.

Following tradition, Jews today eat the same meal. Chametz (leavened bread) can be homemade Matzah, or Matzo in a prepared package. Homemade unleavened bread is thin, crisp, and made with flour and water that's cooked quickly. The table is set with a tablecloth, and small dishes of salt water. Three pieces of Matzah bread are tucked inside a folded napkin. Each person receives a Seder plate (plate that holds six foods; pictured below), and a copy of the Haggadah which is a narrative of the Israelite's Exodus from Egypt. Note that the Seder plate holds bitter herbs, part of a lamb's shank bone, Haroseth that is a mixture of apples, nuts, cinnamon, and wine. Other sections hold lettuce, parsley, and hardboiled egg.

Peter and John had to ensure the lamb they used was one without a blemish, not more than one year old, was properly slaughtered under supervision of the priest, and roasted over an open fire. Historians say families who traveled to Jerusalem purchased the roasted lamb. We are not told if the apostles roasted a lamb or purchased one.

However, the intent of Passover was not to share a meal but to remember the story of God redeeming His people from Egyptian slavery. The room was arranged with floor cushions so everyone could recline at the table. Peter and John would have prepared jars of water, wine, bitter herbs, unleavened bread, a fruit and nut paste, a raw vegetable to dip in a tart dressing, and a bowl of salt in which to dip the egg and bread. They would have placed a basin filled with warm water and a towel on a table for hand-washing. Because the preparation required so much detail, it explained the apostles' asking Jesus where they would eat the Passover so they could ensure they had things prepared on time.

Each food has special significance. The Peroah (roasted lamb) helps to recall the painting of blood on their door frames, and the visit of the death angel. Because Zeroah, (a piece of a roasted lamb's shank bone), is not always readily available today, a poultry neck or wing or matzo ball is substituted today and represents God's outstretched arm. Maror (a bitter herb), usually horseradish, represents the bitterness of slavery. Charoset (a nut-fruit-cinnamon paste) symbolizes the clay their ancestors made for the buildings of Pharaoh. Matzah (a homemade unleavened bread) is dipped into the salt three different times during the meal to symbolize removing arrogance and pride from their souls, and it represents how hastily the people left Egypt. Karpas is lettuce or parsley dipped into saltwater and represents tears shed by the Israelites. Beitzah is a roasted egg that indicates life and a continuation of existence. The egg is often dipped in saltwater. The four cups of wine or grape juice (today) each person consumes is to recall God's promises.

All preparations were completed by 6:00 p.m. when others arrived to begin the meal. The meal was held at night because the people escaping Egypt left at night. Their time differed from our use of a day going from midnight to midnight. The Israelites measured their day from sunset to sunset. (Lev. 23:32). They had a full night and full day. God had commanded the Israelites leaving Egypt to slaughter a lamb just after sunset and to eat it the same night. (Ex. 12:6, 8).

Today, the leader of the meal begins by telling about the blood on the doorposts, and how the first-born killed in Egypt were the first of Ham's sons to reach manhood (Ps. 78:51). The youngest son explains the meal's significance. The leader then retells the entire story of the Exodus from Egypt. For a condensed and beautiful version of how Israel left Egypt read Psalm chapters 105-106-107.

If done according to custom, Jesus and the apostles would have washed their hands before beginning the meal and had a prayer of thanksgiving over the first cup of wine. Next. they dipped the lettuce in bitter herbs. This would be followed with the reading of the Passover Haggadah (events of the Exodus and the first Passover) and the group singing the first part of Hallel (Psalm 113-114).

After singing, each one would break one of their three pieces of bread. Part would be returned to the pile of bread and the other part set aside to be eaten last as dessert. A second cup of wine would begin the main course of roasted lamb. A piece of bread (Matzah) would be dipped in salt and two additional dipping of bread into salt would occur before having the third cup of wine.

The third cup of wine would come with a blessing as the dessert bread was eaten. The celebration would conclude with a prayer, a fourth cup of wine, and singing the rest of Hallel (Psalm 115-118). Below explains how Jesus would have held to this custom.

Before the Passover, Jesus knew the time had come for Him to leave this world and return to His Father. When the hour came (6 pm), Jesus and His apostles arrived and reclined at the table that Peter and John had prepared. He told them, *"I have eagerly desired to eat this Passover with you before I suffer. For I tell you, I will not eat it again until it finds fulfillment in the kingdom of God."* Jesus took the cup of wine and told the others to divide it among themselves. We know it was the first cup of wine, because He always gave thanks before eating.

As the evening meal was served, the devil had already prompted Judas Iscariot to betray Jesus. While eating the lamb, they would have shared the second cup of wine.

Knowing He was returning to His Father, Jesus interrupted His eating to wash His disciples' feet. He didn't want to leave without teaching them that the meaning of love is to be a servant to others. When He came to Peter, who didn't want Jesus washing His feet, He told Peter, *"Unless I wash you,*

you have no part with Me." At that time, it appeared none of the men understood the relationship of His words to being washed clean of sin with baptism. Jesus told them, *"You are clean, though not every one of you,"* because He knew Judas was going to betray Him (Jn. 13:1-12). To comfort them and strengthen their faith, Jesus told His apostles about the coming of the Holy Spirit, His going to be with His Father, and they soon would see Him no longer (Jn. 14:15, 26).

When Jesus said, *"He who shared the bread had lifted up his heel against Me"* He assured the men He was not referring to all of them. It is likely Jesus dipped His bread into the salt water as another dipping was required. What He had said weeks earlier seemed applicable here regarding Judas: *"You are the salt of the earth; but if the salt has become tasteless, how can it be made salty again? It is no longer good for anything, except to be thrown out and trampled underfoot by men"* (Mt. 5:13).

Jesus was troubled in spirit and testified, *"I tell you the truth, one of you is going to betray Me"* (Jn. 13:18-20). Peter motioned for John to ask who Jesus meant. Jesus explained it was the one to whom He would give the piece of bread dipped in the dish. He handed the salted bread to Judas, and Satan immediately entered him. Jesus spoke the Judgement of Judas, *"The Son of Man will go just as it is written about Him. But woe to that man who betrays the Son of Man! It would be better for him if* he had not been born." Judas asked, *"Surely not I, Rabbi?"* Jesus responded, *"Yes, it is you"* (Mt. 26:24-25). Jesus told Judas, *"What you are about to do, do quickly."* Judas took the bread and left, and it was dark outside (Jn. 13:1-27). Once Judas left, Jesus said, *"Now is the Son of Man glorified, and God is glorified in Him.*

The others did not understand what Jesus had said to Judas. Because Judas was in charge of their money, they thought Jesus told him to go buy something for their feast or to give something to the poor (Jn. 13:28-30).

Jesus explained that He would not be with them much longer, and where He was going, they could not come. He gave them a new command, to love one another, as He had loved them.

Jesus took the bread, gave thanks, broke a piece, and gave it to them, saying, *"This is my body given for you; **do this in remembrance of Me"*** (Lk. 22:17, my emphasis).

After the supper concluded, Jesus took the third cup of wine that always came with a prayer of blessing and said, *"Drink from it all of you. **The cup is the new Covenant of my blood**, which is **poured out for many**. I will not drink of this fruit of the vine from now on until that day when I drink it anew with you in my Father's kingdom"* (Mt. 26:27; Lk. 22:20-23 my emphasis). The bread represents Jesus' body and the wine His blood given on the cross for us. His words have a rich, Old

Testament background as related in Exodus (24:8) when Moses took blood and sprinkled it on the people, telling them it was the blood of the Covenant the Lord had made with them.

They would have concluded the celebration by singing a hymn (Ps. 115-118) and drinking the fourth cup of wine. They left the upper room to go to the Mount of Olives (Mt. 26:30; Mk. 14:26). It was at the Mount of Olives where Judas kissed Jesus so the soldiers could identify Him. In a matter of hours, Jesus would be hanging dead on a wooden cross.

Jesus didn't change the Passover, but fulfilled it perfectly by practicing its customary rituals. But He gave it a new meaning. The bread would no longer be about the Israelites being freed from their slavery in Egypt, but about how Christ sacrificed His body that offers us freedom from our slavery to sin. The wine would no longer be about the blood of a lamb on door posts that allowed the angel to pass by without killing the firstborn inside. Wine now represented how the perfect lamb of God had shed His blood on the cross that paid in full the enormous debt we each owe for our sins. Just as the lamb's blood on the door posts saved the life of every first born, Jesus' blood on the wooden cross saves us from sin's curse of hell.

The Lord's Supper is a Covenant celebration and needs to be honored as such, with us knowing that when we gather together, Jesus is present and standing beside us. It is similar to Moses, Aaron, Nadab, Abihu, and the 70 elders celebrating the Covenant at Mt. Sinai with Jesus (Ex. 24:1-10). Otherwise, we risk the Covenant curse of punishment, as Paul told the Corinthians that for one to eat the bread or drink of the cup without recognizing the body of the Lord, he eats and drinks judgment on himself. He further explained that this was why some were weak, sick, and had fallen asleep (died) (1 Cor. 11:30). They had made it a fun time without any reverence shown for the Lord and doing so in a way that excluded and snubbed poor members.

The Lord's Supper is a Covenant celebration and needs to be honored as such

The bread we break is a participation in the body of Christ (1 Cor. 10:16). *Because there is one loaf, we, who are many, are one body, for we partake of the one loaf (v. 17).* This binds us together as fellow-believers in His Church, unlike the Corinthians who partook before all were present and who neglected the poor members, while some got drunk.

The one faithful body is Christ's Church, unified to act and be one as we share how Christ giving His blood signifies our salvation. The cup of thanksgiving for which we give thanks is our participation in the blood of Christ (v.16). We remember the pain He suffered and the reason He volunteered to die for us.

The Lord's Supper serves as a time to renew our commitment to Him, as Paul encouraged the Corinthians to examine themselves before partaking of the feast. The examining was not to determine if they were worthy enough, because none are worthy enough. As the Bible declares: *There is no one righteous, not even one* (Ro. 3:10). Rather Paul was encouraging them to exhibit unity within the Church and to show reverence to how it represents the body and blood of Christ. He was asking the Corinthians to show unity among the church members, strive to gain victory over their own war with sin, and thank the Lord for dying in their place so they could have permanent forgiveness of their wrongs so they are fit for living in heaven with Him.

The Covenant celebration is a time to honor God and edify one another in a celebration of what Jesus has done for us by taking our sin upon Himself. With both thanksgiving, joy, and sadness that our sin cost Jesus such a heavy price, we come to the table each Sunday to remember Christ's sacrifice and proclaim His work for our salvation (I Cor. 11:23-26) and with gladness that He is coming again to bring us to share in His heavenly home.

GODHEAD'S PLAN FULFILLED

God the Father, God the Son, and God the Holy Spirit were consistent in how they implemented their pre-planned Covenants and chose leaders who guided people to obey the Law that led to Christ and our justification by faith (Gal. 3:24). All Covenants focused on the Father's desire to relate to His people, dwell among them, and in them. He does this by strengthening us with power through His Spirit in our inner being so by faith Christ may dwell in our hearts (Eph. 3:16-17).

After Jesus Christ arose from the grave, He appeared to the apostles over a period of 40 days, teaching them and proving to many that He was alive. To grasp the significance of the timing of the changes that occurred requires understanding the importance God placed on the Old Testament Feasts and how each feast marked a significant event in Jesus Christ's life, death, and plan for our salvation.

Passover began on the 14th day of the first month at twilight. The Feast of Unleavened Bread began on the fifteenth day of that month, and for seven days they could eat nothing containing leavening. The sixteenth day of the same month began the Feast of Firstfruits. With the overlapping of multiple feasts, it drew huge crowds that allowed the apostles to begin their teaching to thousands of listeners.

The coordinating of Jesus' life and death with the feasts proved part of the divine plan created in heaven. Jesus was crucified during Passover (Mk. 14:12). His body lay in the grave during the first days of the Feast of Unleavened Bread, and He arose on the Feast of Firstfruits, perfectly fulfilling prophecy.

The Passover retold the Israelites' release from Egyptian slavery and how the lamb's blood on their doorposts, let firstborns escaped death. Christ's death marked our release from the slavery of sin, and with faith in His blood, the Father graces us with escape from the second death of eternal damnation. (Ro. 8:2).

The Unleavened Bread (Lev. 23:6) pointed to Jesus Christ's sinless life. The Bible depicts leavening as sin, so people were not allowed to eat any food that contained leavening during this week. Jesus Christ was the perfect lamb of God, without blemish or defect, making Him the perfect sacrifice to pay our sin debt. (1 Pe. 1:19). He lived a life of perfect obedience (Heb. 4:15).

REQUIRED ANNUAL OLD TESTAMENT FEASTS

Old Testament	Description New	Testament

SABBATH

Ex. 20: 8-11;	Day of rest	Mt.12:1-14;
31:12-17	no work	Mk.2:23-3-5
Lev. 23:3		Lk.4:16-30
Dt. 5:12:15		6:1-10; 13:10-16
		14:1-5; Jn. 5:1-15
		9:1-34;
		Ac.13:14-48; 17:2
		18:4; Heb.4:1-1

PASSOVER

Ex. 12:1-14	Eating lamb	Mt.26:1-2;
Lev. 23:5	w/bitter herbs	Mk.14:12-26;
Num 9:1-14	& bread w/out	Lk.22:7-38
28:16;	yeast	Jn.2:13-25
Dt. 16:1-7		1155-56;
		13:1-30
		1 Cor. 5-7

FIRSTFRUITS

Lev. 23:9-14	Wave offering of	Ro.8:23
	sheaf of first	1 Cor.15:20-23

	barley harvest;	
	burnt offering &	
	grain offering	

PENTECOST (also called Festival of Harvest or of Weeks)

Ex. 23:16a; 34:22	Festival of joy	Ac. 2:1-41;
Lev.23:15-21	voluntary offerings	20:16
1 Num.28:17-25	Firstfruit of wheat	1 Cor.16:8
Dt. 16:9-12	made into 2 loaves	

The Firstfruits Festival required people to bring a bundled sheaf of grain to the priest, who waved it before the Lord. A burnt offering, meal offering, and drink offering were required with the wave offering of grain. No grain could be harvested until the Firstfruits offering was sacrificed to God (Lev. 23).

Scripture uses the word firstfruits to depict faithful believers. Paul called Epaenetus the firstfruit of Achaia, because he was the first of many to be converted in that region. James called believers firstfruits whom Jesus created (1:18), and they are the ones John saw in heaven (Rev.4: 18). *Christ had indeed been raised from the dead, the firstfruits of those who have fallen asleep* (1 Cor. 15:20). Because His resurrection was binding, so will be our resurrection be. Deuteronomy (26: 1-10) explains more of the festival.

During Jesus 40 days on earth after His resurrection, His disciples followed Him, listening to His teachings about the coming kingdom and the necessity of repentance. Jesus was preparing His apostles to assume the role of teaching others. He appeared to them on the first day of the week and showed them His hands and side. He said, *"As the Father has sent me, I am sending you."* And with that He breathed on them and said, *"Receive the Holy Spirit. If you forgive anyone his sins, they are forgiven. If you do not forgive them, they are not forgiven"* (Jn. 20:21-23).

To understand the directive Jesus gave His apostles, we need to remember the reasons Scriptures gave for the Father sending Jesus to earth. The Father sent His Son so that through Him the world might be saved (Jn. 3:17), to speak the words of the Father (Jn. 3:34), to finish the Father's work (Jn. 4:34), to judge only as He hears, and not to please Himself but the Father who had sent Him (Jn. 5:30). Jesus breathed the Holy Spirit on the disciples to ensure they did the same: focused on saving souls, spoke only as told, made judgments that pleased the Father, and remained completely dependent on the Father. The Spirit would help them carry out the commission Jesus had given them, by keeping the focus off themselves. The

Spirit's power centered their thoughts on pleasing the Father, and kept their egos in check. Otherwise, their new abilities might have had them praising and glorifying themselves, not the Father – as we so often do.

To comfort them with His leaving, Jesus explained, *I am going to prepare a place for you. And if I go and prepare a place for you, I will come back, and take you to be with Me that you may be where I am* (Jn. 14:3).

Jesus instructed the apostles not to leave Jerusalem, but to wait for the gift promised by the Father. He told them that while John baptized with water, in a few days they would be baptized with the Holy Spirit. John had told people who came to be baptized by him that Jesus would baptize with the Holy Spirit and fire and separate the wheat from the chaff (Lk. 3:16-18). Now Jesus was sending a guaranteed promise to all believers that they can be part of that great harvest of wheat. That guarantee was and is the Holy Spirit who will be in all who believe in Jesus and are baptized (1 Cor. 12:13; Ac 2:38; 5:32).

One of the last commands Jesus gave the eleven apostles was to make disciples of all nations. (Mt. 28:19-20). He told the Eleven to "*Go into all the world and preach the good news to all creation. **Whoever believes and is baptized will be saved, but whoever does not believe will be condemned*** (Mk. 16:15-16).

Jesus told them to baptize men in the name of the Father, and of the Son, and of the Holy Spirit and to teach them to obey everything He commanded (Mt. 28:19-20).

While with the Eleven, Jesus told them, *"You will receive power when the Holy Spirit comes on you; and you will be my witnesses in Jerusalem, and in all Judea and Samaria, and to the ends of the earth."* After saying this, He was taken up before their very eyes, and a cloud hid Him from their sight (Ac. 1:4-9).

As they stared at the cloud, suddenly two men dressed in white stood beside them. The men asked why they were looking into the sky and told them that Jesus, who has been taken from you into heaven, will come back in the same way you have seen Him go into heaven (Jn. 1:10-11). They had the promise of Jesus' return occurring as suddenly as He had left. Or as Paul says about His returning, *"in a flash, in the twinkling of an eye"* (1 Cor. 15:52).

The Eleven returned to Jerusalem to wait as Jesus had told them. During this time, they replaced Judas with Matthias (Ac. 1:25-26).

When Pentecost came, and they were all together, suddenly, a sound like the blowing of a violent wind came from heaven and filled the whole house. They saw what seemed to be tongues of fire that separated and came to rest on each of them. They were filled with the Holy Spirit and began to speak in other languages as the

169

Spirit enabled them (Ac. 2:1-4). No wonder this grabbed the attention and amazed such a huge crowd of God-fearing Jews who were present from every nation to celebrate the Feasts. Who wouldn't be drawn to see something this unusual?

Note, it was not wind. Scripture does not say they felt air moving against their body or had their hair blown. Rather, it was a sound, and it sounded like the blowing of a violent wind (Ac. 2:2). From heaven, came a loud, can't-ignore-it sound, no matter how hard of hearing one might be. It was violent, as one might expect a wake-up-and-take-note reverberation from heaven. It was as if the Lord blew His breath on them, perhaps, as He had done when He breathed life into Adam.

John (3:8) wrote that you can hear the wind but cannot tell where it is going and so it was with everyone born of the Spirit that day. Those present could attest to John's accurate description. Their baptism with the Holy Spirit was a divine act. The people simply watched God the Holy Spirit appear as tongues of fire and move among them.

In his sermon, Peter pointed out that the promise of the prophet Joel had been fulfilled (Acts 2: 15). *On My menservants and My maidservants, I will pour out My Spirit in those days* (Joel 2: 28-29). Comparable promises can be found in the words of other prophets, such as Ezekiel (36: 27), who prophesied: *I will put My Spirit within you.*

Tongues of fire were not literal hot fire. Scripture says *what seemed to be* tongues of fire (Ac. 2:2). They separated and one rested on each of them. Obviously, no one was burned. Instead, God provided viewers a visual representation of the Holy Spirit's force and power. The appearance of the Holy Spirit produced a visual picture that identified the Holy Spirit's arrival.

Drawing a curious crowd gave Peter and the apostles an opportunity to teach many about Jesus Christ's death and resurrection. With Peter as the primary spokesman, the men described how the Father had raised Jesus to be exalted at His right hand. He told them to **repent** and **be baptized** for the forgiveness of their sins and they would **receive the gift of the Holy Spirit** (Ac. 2:38 my emphasis). Everyone who obeys God by being baptized receives the promised Holy Spirit (Ac. 5:32; 2:38).

What's significant for us about Peter's message of the Holy Spirit, is that he said the Holy Spirit was for them and *"for all who are afar off."* This includes us today. With faith, we are baptized, and we too receive the Holy Spirit, and the Lord adds us to His church.

With faith, we are baptized, and we too receive the Holy Spirit, and the Lord adds us to His Church

That day, 3000 were baptized and the Lord added to the church daily those who were being baptized (Ac. 2:47 KJ). Note that baptism was required before being added by Jesus to His Church. With faith in Jesus, they were baptized, indwelt with the Holy Spirit, and Jesus added them to His Church. John stressed that no one can enter the kingdom of God unless he is born of the water and the Spirit (3:5). When we're **buried in baptism**, Christ circumcises our hearts (Col. 2:12), and the Father forgives all our sins. Any future sins are forgiven and forgotten when we repent. *If we confess our sins, He is faithful and just to forgive us our sins and to cleanse us from all unrighteousness* (1 Jn. 1:9). However, He who covers his sins will not prosper (Prov. 28:13). Repentance carries a sense of remorse for doing wrong and a commitment to change to live by Jesus' commands.

Repentance carries remorse for doing wrong and a commitment to change to live by Jesus' commands

The Bride of Christ is a metaphor used in Scripture to describe Jesus' relationship with His bride, His Church. Portrayed as the bridegroom in this relationship, Jesus reveals Himself to be faithful, loving, and committed to a Covenant union with His Church that's comprised of all who believe in Him and have accepted His atoning grace and gift of salvation. This is the sheep for whom Jesus, the Good

Shepherd cares for, the branches of His vine, and the sons and daughters adopted by the Father (Eph. 1:5).

At baptism, the Holy Spirit joins people to become one with Christ and one with all other believers. Christ lives in us, and our life is no longer ours, but belongs to Him. He takes people with different talents and personalities and unifies them into a single body as His Church. As the Church of Christ, we are a body of two harmonies. The two loafs made of wheat that God required waved symbolized the unity of believing Jews and Gentiles.

The Church is not a building, but a group of believers throughout the world, who know the Lord in a personal, faithful, relationship way. The Spirit lives in each baptized believer, and Jesus says we have the Holy Spirit forever (Jn. 14:16). The body is the one Church begun by Christ, not multiple groups later begun by men. The Bible says He began His Church, not multiple groups that call themselves churches with different beliefs. Paul called the body a unit, made up of many parts that form one body. *For we were all baptized by one Spirit **into one body** -whether Jews or Greeks, slave or free – and we were all given the one Spirit to drink* (1 Cor. 12:13-14 my emphasis).

We are purified by obeying the truth (1 Pe. 1:22), and we are no longer seen by our race, gender, or who our ancestors were. In Christ, we become one body, the Church.

Baptism saves us. Peter (3:21) assures us of this. It's not the removal of dirt from the body, but the pledge of a good conscience toward God. Baptism is our making a Covenant pledge that we will live by God's commands and remain loyal to Him. Striving to keep our conscience clean of sin is why we try to repent of every sin.

The Godhead's perfect timetable of events that fulfilled prophesy happened as they did, and when they did, because it was the day, time, and place planned in heaven before our world was formed. Jesus died as a Passover fulfillment. He rose as a Firstfruits fulfillment. With Firstfruit, Christ guaranteed our resurrection. The Holy Spirit came on Pentecost, as our guarantee of full inheritance of heaven. On Pentecost, Christ added baptized believers to His Church as a Firstfruits fulfillment. All happened on a divine, preplanned timetable.

The Holy Spirit was not a new idea. Previously, many had the Holy Spirit who helped them with special tasks. Such was Saul (1 Sam. 10:6), Moses and the 70 elders (Nu. 11:16-17), Othniel (Jdg. 3:9-10, and many others. However, now, the

Holy Spirit helps as He lives in baptized believers (Ac. 6:5; Ro. 8:9,11; 1 Cor. 3:16, 6:16, 19; Eph. 5:18; 2 Tim. 1:14).

The Holy Spirit could not come until Jesus had been glorified by accomplishing the work the Father had sent Him to earth to do and returned to His Father. When this happened, our eternity was confirmed with His holy promises. It's now up to us to believe He died for us and remain faithful.

As long as we are striving to live obediently, we live heaven-bound. Our inheritance can never perish, spoil, or fade because it is kept secure in heaven by God's power (1 Pe. 1:4).

OUR COVENANT OBLIGATION

Just as the Old Covenant required people to agree to God's stipulations to receive His promises, we too have a requirement for receiving the New Covenant's promises. Jesus described the criteria for the promise and the curse of the New Covenant: *"Whoever believes and is baptized will be saved (Covenant promise), but whoever does not believe will be condemned (Covenant curses' punishment)"* (Mk. 16:16 my emphasis). He asks us to keep our side of the Covenant, and baptism shows that we pledge or promise to live as He asks. Some say faith and repentance are all that is necessary for salvation, but the Lord made it clear that being born again of water and Spirit are necessary to enter the kingdom of God. As Jesus told Nicodemus, you **must** be born again by being baptized (Jn. 3:3,5). To receive the Covenant promise requires all people to be baptized. Those who refuse to obey face the curse's punishment of eternity in hell.

Baptism is symbolic of a death and burial of our sinful self. With our hearts, we believe that Jesus is God's Son who died for us and was resurrected. With our mouth we profess our faith. *Take hold of eternal life to which you were called when you made your good confession in the presence of many witnesses* (1

177

Tim. 6:16). After acknowledging our faith that we believe Jesus is God and the Son of God the Father, who gave his life on the cross for our sins, we are baptized.

Baptism symbolizes Jesus' death, burial, and resurrection. We are fully **immersed** beneath the water, just as Jesus died and was buried. **We rise** out of the water as Christ was raised from the dead **by the Spirit** to the glory of the Father (Ro. 6:4; 8:11). We rise saved **to walk a new life that brings glory to the Lord** and to live eternally with Him. The Father makes us alive with Christ **and forgives all our sins** (Col. 2: 12- 13). All our sins are washed away, never to be remembered again.

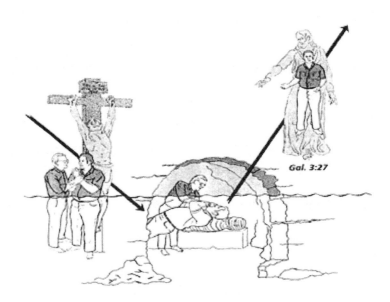

Gal. 3:27

Baptism shows we accept the New Covenant and **pledge to keep a good conscience toward God,** as we strive to live a new life that's dead to sin (1 Pe. 3:2 my emphasis). Paul realized the importance and declared, *"I strive always to keep my conscience clear before God and men"* (Ac.24:16). Note he admitted failing at times (Ro. 7:19), but because he continued trying, he lived saved.

According to a friend who reads the Septuagint, the earliest Greek translation of the Bible from the original Hebrew, the word pledge is found only twice in the Bible. Once in Daniel and the other in First Peter and is translated to mean 'to ask' or to be forgiven when we fail, and to emphasize our part of offering an obedient response. Pledge involves making a promise and working to keep it. Our pledge is our promise to remain obedient to the Lord's teaching and seeking God's help to do so. We pledge to remain faithful, and repent when we fail.

With baptism, we partake of Christ's death, burial, and resurrection (Col. 2:12), as Christ takes on Himself our sins and gifts us with His righteousness (Ro. 5:17). With baptism, we belong to Christ and are made heirs of heaven, according to the Covenant promise.

After being baptized, on the first day of each week, Christ's Church observes the Lord's Supper. Our shared communion with fellow believers had a divine origin and has the intent of remembering what Jesus has done for us. It is all about Jesus Christ, as the bread symbolizes His body that took our sins, and the cup symbolizes the blood He shed for us so we have the Father's forgiveness.

We are told not to forsake the assembling of the Church's body of believers (Heb. 20:25). Jesus knew our attending and fellowshipping with other believers would help us remain faithful. The church's role is evangelism to non-believers and edification for fellow members as we strive to glorify the Father. When most of our friends are faithful believers, we have added support in living as Jesus asks.

Obedience to God's laws and detailed works were the standard for continuing in the Old Covenant. Yet no Israelite could be saved by keeping the Law because no one could perfectly keep words written in stone, nor the 600+ additional requirements. **People are now defined by their relationship to Jesus** (Gal. 3:26-29 my emphasis). Christ's death provided for the peace of our consciences by His blood removing our guilt because of our sins.

Still, obedience is important, just as Jesus was obedient. God will punish those who chosse to ignore His offer of salvation. Christ said, *"If you keep my commandments you will abide in My love, just as I have kept my Father's commandments and abide in His love"* (Jn. 15:10). Obedience proves one's faith is genuine. All believer's sin and fall short of God's glory, but when believers sin, **Jesus** our Mediator, **speaks** to the Father **in our defense** (1 Jn. 2:1 my emphasis). With Jesus defending us and our commitment to change, we can't lose.

The Old Testament was used to advance God's ultimate purpose for all of mankind to be saved by faith. *The **law was put in charge to lead us to Christ so that we might be justified by faith.** Now that faith has come, we are no longer under supervision of the law* (Gal. 3:24-25 my emphasis). The Old Covenant was set aside because it was weak, useless, and made nothing perfect (Heb. 7:18).

The New Covenant is founded on better promises (Heb. 8:6), than the Old Covenant, as was foretold by Jeremiah (31:31-34). It's better because **it writes the Lord's laws on believer's hearts** (Jer. 31:31-34; Heb. 8:8-12 my emphasis). The **Holy Spirit testifies** to us: *"This is the Covenant I will make with them after that time," says the Lord. "**I will put my laws in their hearts, and I will write them on their minds. Their sin and lawless acts I will remember no more"*** (Heb.10:15-17 my emphasis). The Lord confides in those who fear Him; He makes His Covenant known to them (Ps. 25:14).

It's not that God is unable to remember our sins. It's that He chooses to forgive them. He removes our sins from us *as far as the east is from the west* (Ps. 103:12), an immeasurable distance. Genuine forgiveness refuses to recall a wrong.

Through the Spirit's work, all know what is morally and ethically right, and without being taught, all know there is a God who lives (Heb. 8:11). With baptism, God circumcises our hearts with His laws that gives believers an inner will to obey from their love of Him (Ro. 2:29; Heb.8:10-12). The Covenant promises are for people of all ages, past, present, and future, including us today.

You are sons of God the Father through faith in Christ Jesus, for all of you who were baptized into Christ have clothed yourselves with Christ (Gal. 3:27). Because you now belong to Christ you are heirs of the Covenant promise (v.29).

With any sins committed after our baptism, we regret them and seek God's forgiveness. This draws us closer to him and makes us conscious of how easily we can slip and realize our need to grow in His Word. With repentance we claim the Lord's promise of His forgiving and remembering our sins no more (1 Jn. 1:9; Heb. 8:12).

With repentance we claim the Lord's promise of forgiving and remembering our sins no more

With faith in Jesus, baptized believers are recipients of the Covenant promise. We are assured a home in heaven; our citizenship is guaranteed (Phil. 3:20), and Jesus has a special place prepared just for us (Jn. 14:2). Our names are added in the Book of Life (Rev. 3:5). Christ adds us to His Church, and we receive the gift of the Holy Spirit to aid in our walk with the Lord (Ac. 2:47). We are adopted by the Father (Gal. 4:7; Ro. 8:23; Eph. 1:5) and co-heirs with Christ (Ro. 7:17). If you have been baptized and strive to live for Him, Heaven already belongs to you.

Our sins - all sins – past, present, and future are forgiven as long we strive to stay in close fellowship with the Lord. We still sin and are told to repent, but as long as our hearts **believe in Him** and we **strive to obey, we are protected with His grace,** and **Jesus' blood continues cleansing us** (1 Jn. 1:7; Eph. 5:26 my emphasis). As a wise friend once described our condition, "We live saved. We don't fall in and out of God's grace." We have the Holy Spirit living in our hearts to help us obey the Lord's commands (Ro. 5:5; Eph. 3:16; I Cor. 3:16, 6:19; 2 Cor. 1:22). As long as we keep trying, we lived saved and heaven bound!

Under the New Covenant. continuing in unrepented sin earns one the Covenant curse of eternity in Hell. Sin is most often defined as works of the flesh, such as the desires and passions of the body: sexual immorality, idolatry, hatred, discord, jealousy, fits of rage, selfish ambition, etc. Yet, there is not one of these sins that the Lord won't forgive with repentance and change – and He'll remember them no more.

Many who reject the Lord's promises make religious decisions by their emotions, not their intellect from study of God's Word They want immediate pleasure and self-gratification, and living in heaven feels too remote. They create emotional reasons to support their sinfulness. It lets them justify setting their own moral standard of what's right instead of using God's Word. The baptized who fall away **hate Him because the Holy Spirit will convict them of their sinful decisions** (Jn. 15:18 my emphasis). They do not want such selfish self-centeredness exposed, let alone have it condemned.

The baptized who fall away <u>hate Him</u> because the Holy Spirit will convict them of their sinful decisions

Certainly, if man doesn't have faith that Jesus lived and died to save him, he won't be baptized. This man can only expect to receive God's curse by spending eternity in a fiery lake of burning sulfur (Rev. 21:8). The stench of sulfur without a mask or a breath of fresh air will surely be unbearable, but it may be nothing compared to the never-ending fire. Other Scriptures add more descriptors of hell: *The Son of Man will send out His angels, and they will weed out of His kingdom everything that causes sin and all who do evil. They will throw them*

184

into the fiery furnace, where there will be weeping and gnashing of teeth. However, the righteous will shine like the sun in the kingdom of their Father. (Mt. 8:12; 13:41-43,50; 22:13; Lk. 13:30).

Jesus said that **hell's punishment is for the cowardly and unbelieving** who reject Him in favor of worldly pleasures (Rev. 21:8 my emphasis). The irony of pleasure-seeking is that it always leaves us wanting more. We can't climb the ladder of success high enough. Or, travel around the world far enough. Or keep up with society's style changes fast enough. Or get rich enough. All worldly desires leave us with a nagging feeling that we're never satisfied. Only Jesus can show us we are enough. We are loved enough. Wanted enough. . . enough that He died to prove it to us.

Hell is also for those who begin with the Lord and then **stray permanently** from Him (Jn. 15:6; Mt. 13:30 my emphasis). Scripture is firm that **we can fall from grace** (Gal.5:4). Such was the case of Simon. Scripture clearly states that Simon believed and was baptized (Ac. 8:13). However, sometime later, after seeing the apostles perform miracles, Simon wanted to buy that ability. Peter told him that his heart was not right and full of bitterness, and he was captive to sin (v. 21-22). Peter insisted he had to repent of his wickedness and pray to the Lord. We hope he did.

Hebrews (10:26-27) documents, *If we deliberately keep on sinning after we have received the knowledge of the truth, no sacrifice for sins is left, but only a fearful expectation of judgment and raging fire that will consume the enemies of God.* People, who never return to the Lord, share the lake of fire with Satan and his evil spirits. Sadly, many say they will return one day, but their death comes too soon, and their delay results in them spending eternity with horrible companions while experiencing the worse of all possible pain. After one's death, there are no second chances. Delaying is dangerous because John explains: *Man is destined to die once, and after that to face the judgment.* We only get one life to live, and no one will escape appearing before Christ in judgment (Heb. 9:27). The ones who postponed accepting Jesus' offer can only expect to hear, *"I never knew you. Away from Me you evildoers!"* (Mt. 7:23).

The Lord's curses were necessary because many people love their sin more than they love Jesus. This was confirmed when Jesus said people disobey because they hate Him. *"**They hate Me** because I testify that what the world does is evil"* (Jn.7:7 my emphasis). They may argue that they don't hate Jesus, but He declared that their sin proves they do. Wherever Jesus traveled, He stressed that obedience shows we love Him.

Jesus said people disobey because they *hate Me*

While having dinner with a Pharisee host, Jesus told him the more sins we confess, the more we love Him and others (Lk 7:36-50). Once we can admit how sinful we are, the more we realize we deserve hell, and the more we love Jesus because we get heaven instead. The more sins we confess, the more we realize how we are no better than any other sinner. Our sin may differ from our neighbors, but without Jesus, all sin deserves the second death in hell, and yet, because of His sacrifice for us, we can enjoy heaven.

Once we can admit how sinful we are, the more we realize we deserve hell, and the more we love Jesus because we get heaven instead

If we refuse to confess our wrongs, Jesus still knows the sin that lies in our hearts. *Hear from heaven, your dwelling place. Forgive and act; deal with each man according to all he does, since you know the hearts of all men* (1 Ki. 8:39 my emphasis).

Without faith, we cannot please God (Heb. 10:6). Once the heart hardens from continued willful sin, the conscience stops nagging one to change. It means we have put out the fire of the Holy Spirit, and denied the Spirit freedom to work in our lives. Such falling away is very different than the person who stumbles, has times of weakness, or even experiences temporary lapses in their faith, but who by God's grace, returns and seeks God's forgiveness. The question is, *"Do we regret every sin and want to be forgiven and try again?"* If so, we repent - and God forgives and remembers our sins no more.

Those who don't believe in the Lord are condemned already (Jn. 3:18). They continue in their sin for the same reason that David sinned with Bathsheba. David **hated God hated God's word**, and **loved his sin more** (2 Sam. 12:9-10 my emphasis). Despite man's sinfulness, God still wants all to love Him as He loves us. He never stops wanting us to live eternally with Him in His heavenly home. He never stops loving all He created, but He cannot allow sin into heaven or it wouldn't be Paradise.

God won't control us. He never withdraws our free will. By misusing our freedom, we receive God's curse as the Israelites did who continued in disobedience. We can turn away from the Lord, and delight in sin until our heart hardens beyond the Holy Spirit's reach, but it is us who left the Lord. He never abandons us, and He welcomes home every repentant child.

Those who fall away and remain unrepentant have only a promise of the curse of an unfathomable eternity in hell. They know better. God put His morals in their hearts. They are without excuse.

If hardened ones will repent and return, the Father delights in the wayward prodigal's coming home, so much so, He races to welcome home His disobedient child who wants to change (Lk. 15:11-32). The Father is so joyful over the return of His once lost child, He throws a party with the angels in heaven to honor the repentant one's decision to come home (Lk.15:10).

Our requirement is having faith that Jesus is God's Son, who died for our sins, being baptized, striving to keep our pledge. By doing this we can cling to His promise of resurrecting us from the dead to live eternally with Him. Jesus' exhortation to *make every effort* to enter the narrow gate is a command to repent when we sinfully live by our own standard instead of Jesus' commands, and strive to remain faithful so God can grant us entrance. God's requirement is so simple and easy that most miss it.

Christ's sacrifice on the cross made perfect **forever** those who are being made holy (Heb. 10: 14). Note that Scripture says '*who are being made holy,*' not who were. This is another reminder that the New Covenant was created for faithful believers throughout all ages. We are continually in need of His forgiveness because everyone continues to sin. Thankfully, He ensured that we know how to receive full and total forgiveness if we break our pledge to keep a clean heart. It's why the Lord's forgiveness is such a monumental blessing.

As Paul explained, *"You have been set free from sin and have become slaves to God, the benefit you reap leads to holiness, and the result is eternal life"* (Ro. 6:22).

HOLY SPIRIT

The Holy Spirit is God and One of the Holy Godhead: God the Father, God the Son, and God the Holy Spirit. The LORD our God, the LORD is One (Dt. 6:4). They are One God in divine essence and three in person, as they think as one, act as one, and live in perfect union. Each possess all that is essential to deity and retains His own attributes. All are eternal. We are born of water and of the Spirit when immersed in water for the remission of sins (Jn. 3:5).

Hebrews confirms that the Holy Spirit is eternal like Jesus and the Father (9:14). The Holy Spirit speaks (Ac. 8:29), convicts us of sin to have us change (Jn. 16:8), can be grieved (Eph. 4:30), can be lied to (Ac. 5:3-4), helps us makes decisions (Ac. 15:28), gives us special talents (1 Cor. 12:11), can change one's plans (Ac. 16-6, and reminds us of God's commands (2 Cor. 3:3). Jesus asked His Father to give us a Counselor to be with us forever – the Spirit of truth who will live with us and will be in us (Jn. 14:15-17).

Peter affirms: *"No prophecy was ever produced by the will of man, but holy men spoke from God **as they were carried along by the Holy Spirit*** (2 Pe. 1:21 my emphasis). Our Holy Bible was written by men as they were led by the Holy Spirt. As the

Spirit said, *"I have put My **words in your mouth"** (Jer. 1:9 my emphasis) The sword of the Spirit is the word of God (Eph. 617). That's all the more reason we should study our Bibles.

We are baptized with the Holy Spirt (Ac. 1:5; Mt.3:11) who works in us in personal ways, according to our needs. He is the believer's guarantee of heaven. *God put the Holy Spirit in our hearts as **His seal of ownership** on us **and** as **a deposit, guaranteeing what is to come** (2 Cor. 1:21 my emphasis). He's the Father's seal and promise that we belong to Him. God puts the Spirit in our hearts when we are baptized. The whole of God is continually with us, wherever we are, and at all times. With the **Spirit living in our inner being,** God dwells continually in our hearts through faith (Eph. 3:17 my emphasis).

When we unite ourselves with the Lord, we are one with Him in Spirit. Our body becomes a temple of the Holy Spirit as He lives inside us (1 Cor. 3:16). In the Old Testament, the temple was where God met with the priest, making it a holy place because God's Spirit dwelt there. As His temple today, we become a holy body and need to take special care of ourselves—spiritually, physically, and emotionally. That's why we should not take anything unclean into our bodies, or use the body to sin, but rather, discipline our hearts and minds to stop reacting to sin's temptations. God loves our bodies and doesn't want them polluted by fleshly lusts. To think, *"It's my body, and I will do whatever I want with it"* is to show a combative spirit. How we care for our bodies displays the respect we have for it, as something bought and paid for with the blood of Christ on Calvary's cross. The Old Testament temple was built for worshipping the Lord, and today, God calls us, His temple, to worship Him by spending time talking with Him, studying His Word, and sharing with fellow believers in worship. We are told to present our bodies as a living and holy sacrifice, because this is our spiritual service of worship (Ro. 12:1).

A work of the Holy Spirit is to convict us of our sins and press us to remain faithful. Jesus said, *"He will convict the world of sin, and of righteousness, and of judgment"* (John 16:8). The Holy Spirit uses many sources to have us realize our sins: a terrible accident, a mother's prayers, a shocking sermon. Or as Job (33:14-22) describes: in a dream, vision, deep sleep, terrifying incidents, hastening pain with constant distress in our bones, our flesh wasting away to nothing until our bones stick out, or to the point of death. The Mediator (Jesus) tells this sick man what he needs to do and that is to pray (v. 26), and then the man can say, *"I did not get what I deserved. He redeemed my soul from going to the pit, and I will live to enjoy the light"* (v. 27,28). Job says God knows the motives of men's hearts and thoughts. Nothing is hidden from the Spirit. He exposes man's sins and convicts his heart to turn his soul back from the pit so that the light of life may shine on him (30). He pulls at our consciences so we feel deserved guilt and realize our need to change.

The Holy Spirit works in us individually and in the Lord's Church as a group of believers by creating fellowship among the members instead of fractions (Ac. 4:32). *Those who believed were of one heart and soul.* The Spirit creates in each member a love and devotion for one another, and a desire, as an individual and as a group, to convert the world. The believer's command is not to put out the Spirit's fire by suppressing His ministry, but to listen as He points out our need to repent and help others.

God, the Holy Spirit, is present everywhere. No matter where we live or travel, He is present. *Where can I go from Your Spirit? Or where can I flee from Your presence?* (Ps. 139:7). The Holy Spirit lives in your heart, and He lives in my heart (Ac. 6:5; Ro. 8:9-11; 1 Cor. 3:16, 6:16; 2 Cor. 1:22; Eph 5:18; 2 Tim. 1:14). His work is personal and intimately designed for what we each individually needs. If we are at opposite ends of the earth, He is in all who have been baptized and who strive to live by the Covenant pledge. God has poured His love into our hearts by the Holy Spirit, whom He has given us (Ro. 5:5), and *we love because He first loved us (1 Jn. 4:19).* With the Holy

Spirit's help, we can learn to love the Lord with all our heart, soul, mind, and strength as commanded and love others. Our love of Jesus' commands begins in our hearts with help from the Holy Spirit. Our hearts hold our values and motives which are designed to keep our souls pure. Our values direct hou we think in our minds which then determines how we act or use our strength, both physically, emotionally, and spiritually. If we listen to the Holy Spirit, we live right by God's standard and can learn to love the Lord with all our heart, soul, mind, and strength. If we do wrong, the place to begin correction is with the values in our heart.

God will never break His Covenant promise. We can nullify God's eternal promise with continued rebellion, but God can't. He promised, and He cannot lie. The Holy Spirit testifies with our spirit that we are God's child, and He will raise us from the dead like He raised Christ from the dead. We will become **co-heirs with Jesus and receive the Spirit of son-**

ship that allows us to call our Holy Father the personal, intimate title of Abba (Ro. 8:11-15 my emphasis).

As my husband and I rode a bus in Italy, the young boy in front of us kept trying to grab his father's attention who was talking with another. The boy pleaded, *"Abba, listen to this. Listen, Abba! Let me tell you this, Abba."* That's how close the Spirit draws us to the Father. God welcomes us calling for His attention at any time and in any place. He wants us to feel so close to Him that we think nothing of calling Him with the smallest reasons. Yet, we must never lose our respect and fear of the Lord, just as the young boy on the bus showed his father. When the father grasped the young boy's shoulder with a firm hand, the boy quietly waited until the men finished talking. The father then turned to his son to hear his childish story. Because we are Abba's heavenly adopted children, His influence over us is as powerful. As this boy's earthly father is jealous for him and angry if he's hurt by another, so our heavenly father is jealous for us because of the esteemed value he holds for each of us.

The Holy Spirit gives us **the power and ability to witness to others about Jesus'** life, death and resurrection (Ac. 1:8). Telling others about Jesus is the last thing Jesus said to His disciples before he ascended into heaven, and being baptized we become a disciple too (Ac 1:8). No matter how shy or fearful we may be, the Holy Spirit helps us find another with whom we are capable of sharing the Good News. *For **God did not give us a spirit of timidity**, but a spirit of power, of love, and of self-discipline* (Tim. 2:7). When we are willing, He provides a person with whom we can share.

God saves us, not because of righteous things we do, but because of His mercy. ***He saves us through the washing of rebirth (baptism) and renewal by the Holy Spirit,*** *which He poured out on us generously through Jesus Christ our Savior* (Tit. 3:5 my emphasis). With baptism, we are born again spiritually by the Spirit as He changes us from being spiritually defeated and facing eternal hell to becoming one that's holy and assured of eternal life.

Salvation is only the beginning of our Christian walk. Our goal is to become Christ-like, and the Holy Spirit's work is to make us into a new person, a born-again person, who becomes more and more like Jesus Christ so we represent Him well on earth (Col. 3:5-10). Being Christlike is letting Christ reign in our hearts so He shines so strong in our lives that people are drawn to Him. When people look at you, do they think what a good person you are, and if they say so, do you tell them it is because of Jesus and what He has done for you?

The Holy Spirit is the Spirit of truth, and speaks what He hears from the Lord, helping us know how to live as the Lord would have us. *We all, who with unveiled faces contemplate the Lord's glory, are being transformed into His image with ever-increasing glory, which comes from the Lord, who is the Spirit"* (2 Cor. 3:18).

Jesus said the Holy Spirit would not speak of Himself, but He comes to magnify and glorify Jesus Christ by helping us remember all Christ has done for us (John 16:13-14). Jesus said, *"The Helper, the Holy Spirit, whom the Father will send in my name, will teach you all things and bring to your remembrance all that I have said to you"* (Jn. 14:26). When we read the Scriptures and suddenly understand the meaning of a verse we have previously missed, we see Him working in our lives. The sword of the Spirit is the word of God (Eph. 6:17). We grow in the knowledge of Jesus Christ, by help of the Holy Spirit.

Jesus gave men Spiritual gifts, as apostles, prophets, evangelists, pastors, and teachers **to establish His Church** *and to help prepare us* **to know how to serve His Church** (Eph. 4:12 my emphasis). We still learn from these men today as we study their writings. Once baptized, the Holy Spirit gives us areas of service we can each best do, ***gifts of the Holy Spirit are distributed according to Jesus' will*** *(Heb. 2:4 my emphasis). He helps us develop those gifts* **for increasing unity in Jesus' Church**, (I Cor. 12:7-11 my emphasis). We strive to rid our sinful desires and live holy lives by living by the Spirit's fruit of love, joy, peace, longsuffering, kindness, goodness, faithfulness, gentleness, self-control, the moral character traits valued for serving Christ's body, His Church (Gal. 5:22-23).

As we endure trials, God's love is poured into us through the Spirit, and with this empowerment He carries us through difficult times. *May the God of hope fill you with all joy and peace in believing, so that* **by the power of the Holy Spirit you may abound in hope** *(Ro. 15:13 my emphasis).* Hope is possible through the power of the Holy Spirit because we know whom we can rely on and never have to bear burdens alone.

He helps us word prayers that we find too difficult to express. *We do not know what to pray for as we ought, but the* **Spirit himself intercedes for us** *with groaning too deep for words* (Ro. 8:26 my emphasis). He speaks to the Father for us when we feel so overwhelmed, we don't know the right words. A parent who has a child struggling with cancer understands His help well.

He warns us of Spiritual dangers and pitfalls that can cause us to stumble. Heeding such warning, however, is up to us. Ask any drug addict who overcomes his addiction by replacing every sinful urge immediately with prayer for God to intervene and stop his craving. At first, he lives in constant prayer, but eventually he finds himself praying less about his addicted craving and more about other needs.

He protects us from physical harm, just as He does spiritual harm, and I believe the angels help (Heb. 1:14; Ps. 34:7, 91:1-11). While living in Delaware, we often took a shortcut road to a great pastry shop. This time as we were headed home, I felt an overwhelming need to return a different way. I told my husband that I could not explain why, but I desperately wanted him to go the long way home. He did it to appease me, and the following morning our newspaper showed wreckage of two cars who had crashed on the shortcut road. Both cars had overturned into the wide, deep stream that ran beside the road. All were killed. I believe this intense urging was because God wasn't yet finished with us.

With the Holy Spirit's help, we can do as Paul did and press on to take hold of the promises God offers. Just like a prior addict, we can *forget what is behind and strain forward as we press on for the goal to win* the prize for which the Father has called us heavenward in Christ Jesus (Col. 3: 12-14). Our Holy Father will never withdraw His offer. His promise is eternal.

Our inheritance can never perish, spoil, or fade because it's being kept securely in heaven by our heavenly Father's power (1 Pe. 1:3). We are to cling tightly to our confidence, and it will be richly rewarded (Heb. 10:35).

DYING TO SELF

With baptism, we feel God's love. It is a warm emotion of thankfulness that all our sins are forgiven. Our fear of hell is gone, we have a sense of knowing God, and an assurance that heaven awaits us. However, we are also aware that we must stop focusing on our sinful desires, and now focus on how God would have us live. We cannot set our own moral standards that differs from Jesus' or challenge His authority and be saved. While once enslaved to sinful pleasure, now that we know the truth, we are not to stray from His word or take His grace for granted. We are to work to replace sin with godliness. Paul described this best: *Since you have been raised with Christ, set your hearts on things above, not on earthly things. Your life is now hidden in Christ, and you will appear with Him in glory.* **Put to death whatever belongs to your earthly nature** (Col. 3: 1-5 my emphasis). Believers continue the process of purification and perfection throughout their entire lives. Striving to cleanse our hearts and souls shows faith and produces hope in God's promises (1 Jn. 3:3). John taught that everyone who has hope purifies himself (1 Jn. 23:3).

We are to die to self (deny self) and take up our cross daily and follow Jesus (Mt. 16:25). We give up (deny self) all that takes our focus off living as Jesus asks. To put our desires above Jesus' commands has us worshipping ourselves. We are to set aside our desires and live the life God planned for us. Jesus said when a seed falls to earth and dies, it then bears much fruit ((Jn. 12:24; Gal. 5:22-23). We are to die to self-will and live by God's will, bearing fruit that brings the Father glory. This frees us from a life of self-absorption and selfishness and makes us a kinder, nicer friend. Too often, we think we are capable and can be successful on our own, and we pray only when facing huge, stressful situations. Self-focus instead of God-focus is idolatry. It has us worshipping ourself, and that's repulsive to God. How He must detest man's arrogance.

A desire for holiness must become our goal when we profess to love the Lord, because it is not enough just to believe. Many believe Jesus died for them. The even attend church services, but they do not practice their faith. Jesus has always detested human efforts to please Him by keeping ritual acts while failing to obey His moral laws (Isa. 65:3). Continuing in willful sin will cost them their souls (Heb. 10:26).

To know the Lord is to love Him (Mt. 22:37-38), and to love Him is to live trying to please Him (Jn. 14:15). The more we read His word, the better we know Him. We don't love strangers. If we fail to fill our hearts with His word, Satan will slowly dominate hearts that were once cleansed and pure.

We are to make serving the Lord our life purpose. Otherwise, we focus on self and have periods when we forget or neglect Him. If we are a truck driver, physician, homemaker, or whatever job, we must make our career secondary to serving the Lord. We can be a Christian first as we work at being an attorney, or carpenter, or waitress. No matter our daily tasks, we behave, and speak as for God, not man.

While teaching college students, I was fortunate that I could use Biblical examples to prove psychological points, such as how we remember facts longer if we put them to music or they rhyme. The apostles' song was a perfect example because it does both. But I knew if even one student complained about my use of the Bible, I could be fired. My husband supported me and removed my concern when he said, *"If they fire you, it is for such a good cause, you should be proud, not upset. You don't have to work, so do what you know is right."* Instead of being in trouble, during the last day of class,

I received notes from students thanking me for teaching them to do what's right. How I cherish their comments.

The foundation on which we are to build all areas of our lives is to be Jesus Christ (1 Cor. 3:11). *Salvation is found in no one else, for there is no other name under heaven given to men by which we must be saved* (Ac. 4:12). Money won't save us. Recreation won't save us. Our family can't save us. A career cannot save us. Only Jesus does that. *He that believes that Jesus is God's Son who died for us and is baptized will be saved* (Mk. 16:16).

All mankind is the object of God's love, but Christians are loved in a special, unique way. They have a host of angels that serve God by supporting faithful humans with what they need to keep going (Heb. 1:14). The angel of the LORD encamps all around those who fear Him (Ps. 34:7). He gives His angels charge over you to keep you in all your ways. In their hands they shall bear you up (Ps. 91:1-11). Ministering spirits (angels) are sent forth to minister for those who will inherit salvation (Heb. 1:14). Even with such help, new Christians cannot instantly make all needed improvements.

Few new converts recognize the ways they need to change until learning more truth and developing a deeper faith. It's their duty to obey what they know and cultivate the habit of learning more as they replace prior sins by doing good deeds for others. It's how they can keep Satan away. However, they also need to prepare for Satan tempting them with sinful desires they once enjoyed, and planting doubts in their minds about the Lord's love and forgiveness. Satan wants new converts to waste their confession and turn back to a world of sin. Believers need to seek God's help like David sought: *Keep your servant from willful sins; may they not rule over me. Then will I be blameless and innocent of great transgressions* (Ps. 19:13).

For a new believer, it often seems there's little left that's good. Sinful activities dominate society and run rampant in our schools and government. Instead of teaching that sex outside of marriage is sinful, parents allow schools to teach kindergarten children how to perform sexual acts. Many dress young girls in ways to sexualize them and then wonder why sexual trafficking of children is among the most profitable of illegal trades. Some politicians work to legalize actions God condemns. We can no longer scan TV without seeing someone dressed in skimpy underwear, or having sex, or hearing God's name profaned. Television has become a protected playground for Satan, and many continue to stare. Worse is when we hear people boast of their sinfulness, (e.g. bragging about cheating others, living together without marriage, etc.). *When we boast of our sin, we are a disgrace in the eyes of God* (Ps. 52:1), *and He will bring us down to everlasting ruin* (v. 5).

As Paul described, *"There is no fear of God before their eyes"* (Ro. 3:18). Jesus warned, *"Because of the increase of wickedness, the love of most will grow cold"* (Mt. 24:12). Satan is at work in all who are disobedient and follow the world's standards (Eph. 2:1-2), and such people are storing up wrath for themselves and will pay in full -- forever-- for their sins (Ro. 2). They have dismissed thoughts of judgment and punishment from their minds, until such fear has passed. As C. H. Spurgeon is noted to say: *"They think they can live fine without the Lord, but they cannot afford to die without Him."*

Only when we learn to hate the things God hates, have we learned to revere and fear Him. Sinful living will never be God's standard, nor the standard for any who are accepted into heaven. Once we wear Christ's name (Christian), we must be striving to live by His moral laws, not conforming to a sin-saturated world. *The Lord knows those who are His,* and *everyone who confesses the name of the Lord must turn away from wickedness* (2 Ti. 2:19).

We cannot conform to the image of Christ and to the image of the world. We cannot have it both ways. James (4:4) says friendship with the world is hatred toward God. We must learn to say no: *"Thank you, but I can no longer do that because I have accepted Jesus as my Lord and Savior."*

Believers are commanded to be transformed by the renewing of their minds and present their bodies as a living sacrifice ((Ro. 12:1-2). While this includes our entire bodies, it seems our mouths are the most challenging body part to control (Js. 3:6). *The tongue is a fire, a world of evil among the parts of the* body (Js. 3:6). We say things we regret and say them in ways that prove offensive. To me, the worst appears to be how so many use their mouth to defame the Lord's holy name.

All sins hurt God, and *every* sin abuses His holy name and His status. Recall when Moses asked to see God's glory, how God began His walk-by repeating His name twice, saying the LORD, the LORD. That's how important God considers His name because His name reflects His reputation, His character. When we hear another's name, we immediately recall what we know about the person 's reputation, and so it is with the Lord's name.

God told the house of Israel, *"I am going to do these things, but for the sake of My holy name. I will show the holiness of My great name, which has been profaned among the nations, the name you have profaned among them"* (Eze. 36: 22).

When we think of God's name being used as a routine, common word, we think of profanity or used in flippant ways. I had a boss who habitually said, *"My God. . ."* Finally, I could no longer stand hearing this, and I asked, *"Are you praying or profaning God's name?"* His face reddened and never again did he repeat it in my presence.

To profane God's name verbally is to make it a common, typical word rather than honoring it with the fearful reverence that's due Him. Scripture teaches we will be judged by our every idle word (Mt. 12:36). To blaspheme God's name verbally is to speak of Him with contempt or to cause others to think of Him in ways that discount His holiness. Any way that devalues God's goodness, shows contempt for Him, blasphemes His holy name, or insults His reputation is sinful. Recall that Jesus taught by example to treat His Father's name as holy, making it first in importance in what we call the Lord's Prayer, by opening with *Hallowed be Thy name.* In Malachi, He warns, *"If you do not set your heart to honor My name, I will send a curse upon you (2:6)."* The Lord will not hold anyone guiltless who misuses His name (Ex, 20:7).

Satan is the one who motivates man's evil uses of God's name and reputation. His involvement is easily recognized. When people swear, and try to sound tough by telling another to go to hell, they speak of the Covenant's cursed place where Satan and unbelievers are condemned. Notice that such people never use Satan's name for swearing. Instead, they use the names of God and Jesus that Satan hates. However, even when Satan tempts people to use our Lord's holy name in irrelevant ways, he is admitting that God exists and that heaven and hell are real. Remember, while Jesus walked the earth, it was Satan's evil spirits who recognized Jesus was the Son of God, and they admitted knowing Jesus had authority and power over them (Mt. 8:29-31; Mk. 1:23-27). If you misuse God's name, do you realize Satan is controlling your mind?

Scriptures confirm that every sin we commit brings shame and contempt for God's name and reputation, and it's not just vulgar words. For example, giving one's child to an idol profaned God's name (Lev. 18:21). Wouldn't it be the same to teach our children there is no God or to raise them believing teachings that contradict His Holy Word?

In addition, Christians are told there must not be even a hint of sexual immorality, or any kind of impurity, or greed because they are improper for God's holy people. *No immoral, impure, or greedy person - such a person is an idolater - has any inheritance in the kingdom of Christ and of God.* Nor should there be obscenity, foolish talk, or coarse joking, which are out of place. We are commanded not to be partners with people who do such things (Eph. 5:3-7). For example, Israel's unfaithfulness to God was not only a form of spiritual prostitution, but it led to numerous people committing the sexual acts themselves. God was so displeased He scattered their dead bodies all over the dessert (1 Cor. 10:5). Their behavior belittled God's reputation with their neighbors. Jews were told they blasphemed His name among the Gentiles by how they acted (Ro. 2:24). They had no influence for bringing neighboring groups to the Lord.

There are many sinful behaviors given in Scripture that are described as profaning His holy name other than our words, sexual sins, and vulgarity. For example, the following sins profane God's name and reputation: stealing (Prov. 30:9), harlotry (Eze. 43:7), a man and father having sex with the same girl (Amos 2:7), swearing falsely (Lev. 9:12), treating ourselves as wiser than God and thinking we can do things our way (Ge. 3:6-7), breaking our vows (Dt. 23:21), offering second rate sacrifices when we have first-class ones we could offer (Mal. 1:10), viewing the Lord's table with contempt (Mal. 1:12); and when we marry someone who worships a foreign god (Mal 2:11). Such dishonorable behaviors should make us tremble. For baptized believers, it should make us aware of how seriously He takes our pledge to Him of keeping a good conscience (1 Pe. 3:21). Because God is holy, His holiness should be the image we leave in the thoughts of others.

Deuteronomy (6:7-8) tells how we can learn to keep the Lord's ways continually in our thoughts. We talk with Him before we begin our day and as we lie down each evening. We talk about Him during the day and post Scriptures for support. The more we talk to Him and about Him, the more our hearts are filled with His love and appreciation for all He does for us.

I know a woman who taught her children about the Lord by constantly applying Deuteronomy (6:7-8) to almost everything she did with them? If it was a raining, she thanked Him for watering the earth and discussed rain's importance. At night, she reminded how God has named every star and how they help men navigate at sea. At the zoo, she described how Jesus created the animals before making man and why everything was perfect before man was created and how man is the only created being with a soul. With a rainbow, she explained why men needed such a symbol. If she stopped for a red light, she discussed how laws keep us safe and how God's commands keep us safe and protect us from hell. When trees changed colors, she reminded how the world always evolves through repeated seasons and in the same order year after year and the many ways this helps men make plans and know God's in constant control. That's the type training God expects of parents because it keeps the love of God in the parent's heart and in the children's hearts. And that's the type parents who are more likely to enjoy eternity with their kids.

Dying to self means we not only sacrifice to God our mouth and words (Eph. 4:29-32), but our entire body. It has to include our egos, and that requires removing multiple layers of selfishness, but it's an essential part of our sanctification. Dying to our self-will (denying self) and living by God's will has to become our goal. Our entire life is to be a sacrifice for the Lord, and when it is, He returns bountiful blessings.

We sacrifice our eyes to Him by carefully selecting what we agree to see or reject (1 Jn. 2:16; Mt. 6:22), our hands by what we touch (Prov. 6:17; 1 Ti.2:8), attitudes by how we are when with others (Eph. 4: 23; Ro. 15:5, 12:16), feet by where we go and refuse to go (Eph. 6:15), and our hearts by valuing His moral commands (Prov. 4: 23-24). Doing this with all parts of our body has us learning to love God as each part learns to do what's right, and we realize the tremendous amount of strength it takes to say no to many desires. God will always supply the strength we need when it is used to serve Him. Our minds grow strong with study of His word, our souls stay pure by practicing repentance, all which ensure our hearts overflow with love for Him and others. Like Paul, we discipline *all* of our body so we are qualified in His sight (1 Cor. 9:27). Then we learn to love Him with our hearts, souls, minds, and strength.

Dying to self is one of the most difficult challenges a believer confronts. We stand before the Lord as helpless creatures, trusting Him to care for our every need better than we can, and learning to relax and letting Him. We do as He says, no matter our inclination to do otherwise, just as Abraham went, not knowing where He was going. It's forcing ourselves to be humble and caring about others' desires too. We strive to learn to love the moral values the Holy Spirit pushes us to live by.

Such change requires spending many quiets times in talks with the Lord, asking Him to show us areas in our life we have yet to surrender to Him, and for His grace to meet our inner struggle that such change demands (Gal. 5:17; Eph. 5:12). We work to train ourselves to be godly (1 Ti. 4:7) and sanctify Christ as (the only) Lord in our hearts (1 Pe. 3:15). We strive to pray like David: *Keep your servant from willful sin; may they not rule over me. Then will I be blameless, innocent of great transgression* (Ps. 19:13). There is not room in a heart for two lords. We must choose God or self. This requires having a faith than can pray, *'not my will, but thine'* and know that putting Him before all else is worth our struggles.

Our names are written in God's Book of Remembrance when we fear the Lord, esteem His name, keep His reputation pure, help others, and do our best to keep Him first in our lives. The Lord attends to us as we press on toward the goal to win the prize for which God calls us heavenward in Christ Jesus (Phil. 3:14). As He watches us striving to renew our inner being, God promises: *"They will be Mine"* (Mal. 3:17).

OUR LIFE PURPOSE

O ften, we act as if Jesus created us so He and others could honor us. How we cherish being applauded and noted. We boast about our good works. We hang banners on our walls and display trophies on our shelves. How upside down, inside out, and backwards we tend to live. Too often we fail to honor the Lord because self gets in the way. We need to rethink who is due the praise for all we accomplish. We are not the center of the universe. God is. We're not even to be a central focus of our family. God is.

Scriptures tells us that the Father brought all His sons and daughters from the ends of the earth, all who call on His name, **all** He formed and made, and **created for His glory** (Isa. 43:6-7 my emphasis). We were created to glorify the Father in everything we say and do. The key to fulfilling our purpose in this life is discovering the person we were created to be, admitting the talents we were blessed with, finding ways to use them that helps others, and ensuring how we use them brings honor to the Father. The most important way to glorify the Father is by believing that Jesus Christ is the Messiah. Without believing in Jesus, we cannot glorify the Father (Jn. 4:23-24, 14:6).

The key to fulfilling our purpose in this life is discovering the person we were created to be, admitting the talents we were blessed with, finding ways to use them that helps others, and ensuring how we use them brings honor to the Father

Psalm (115:1) explains why we are to glorify the Father: *Not to us, O Lord, not to us, but to Your good name be the glory, because of Your love and faithfulness.* 'Not to us," tends to be ignored, although it's given twice to ensure we recognize the significance of us not taking credit for what we do. The greatest sin may be refusing to give our Holy Father the glory and attempting to honor ourselves. Taking praise God deserves may be a maximum wrong. Recall how Moses took God's glory for himself by letting the people credit him for water pouring from the rock and how it cost Moses the joy of entering the Promised Land. He was Jesus' special friend, and still he was punished for taking praise that rightly belonged to God.

I am the LORD; that is my name! I will not give my glory to another or my praise to idols (Isa. 42:8). *How can I let myself be defamed? I will not yield my glory to another* (Isa. 48:11). We have worthwhile achievements only because of Christ Jesus who has become for us wisdom from God. *Therefore, no one is to boast before the Father, but let him who boasts, boast in the Lord* (1

Cor. 1:26-31). John says our boasting of what we have and what we do comes – not from the Father – but from the world (1 Jn. 1:16). Boasting about oneself is condemned by Jude (1:16). The Father is not going to allow us to take credit for what He does, as if we do things by our own talent, wisdom, or power, instead of by Him gifting us with blessings of these.

While baptism saves us by our faith in Jesus Christ and the Father's loving grace, we are obligated to do our best to honor our Covenant pledge of keeping a good conscience toward God (1 Pe. 3:21). Our pledge requires that we use whatever gifts we have received from our Father to serve others in ways that have them knowing Him. We do this with the strength the Father provides, so He is praised through Jesus Christ (1 Pe. 4:10-11), not us praised.

When Jesus came to earth, He was not seeking honor for Himself but honor for His Father (Jn. 8:50). Jesus glorified His Father by completing the work He was sent to do, and we can do the same because each person is blessed with talent that is to be used for bringing honor to the Father.

Our only real purpose is to glorify the Father by how we live and credit our accomplishments to Him

Jesus taught, *"Let your light so shine among men that they may **see your good deeds and praise your Father** in heaven"* (Mt. 5:16 my emphasis). Jesus criticized Pharisees for wanting the most important seat in the synagogue and greetings in the marketplace (Lk. 11:43). Jesus' goal has always been for mankind to glorify His Father, not think of ourselves too highly.

I will remember forever the time that left me gloating like the Pharisee Jesus described. I was asked to attend a meeting at the last minute, and had to buy my airplane ticket at the airport. Arriving late, I was told I had purchased the last ticket and should take the only remaining seat. Boarding the full plane, I saw one empty seat in first class. Thinking this was the last remaining seat, I sat down feeling proud I had a seat better than if I had been able to prebuy my ticket on line. However, minutes later as I sat gloating, the stewardess informed me I was to take the only seat remaining in tourist class. I was terribly embarrassed. I wished I could turn and run from the plane, rather than march to the back. Everyone's eyes glared at me, probably thinking I was a fool who had tried to cheat. That walk to the back of the plane put my ego in its rightful place. Jesus would not need to correct me again because of thinking too highly of myself for having something better than I deserved.

We are to do works that benefit others, and the Father is to get the praise. It's as simple as that: We help others because serving and using our talents is a part of our Covenant obligation, and the Father receives the glory because He supplies us with the skills and resources we use. If we appreciate what Jesus has done for us, we want to help others. Remember, Jesus demonstrated love by washing the apostles' feet. So, the next time we feel smug about something we have done, and we fail to credit the Lord, we would do well to re-read how God reminded Job what limited abilities he had without the Lord (38-42). Compared to the Lord, Job - like us - had nothing to brag.

We are to do works that benefit others, and the Father is to get the praise.

It's not that the Father needs man's praise; it's that the more we show others His goodness, the more they will want to know Him and live eternally with Him too. Such service helps fulfill the Godhead's plan, designed before the beginning of time, to include all of mankind as a member of Their family. But we must remember we are only to become a *tiny part* of the family, not the Head.

Colossians (3:17 my emphasis) says: *Whatever you do, whether in word or deed, do it **all** in the name of the Lord Jesus, **giving thanks to God the Father through Him.*** If we could learn to apply this command and have all words and actions bring praise to the Father, it would keep our focus on making the Lord first in our lives and stop preoccupation with self. In

219

fact, it may be the only way we can stop our constant thoughts of what we want, how we feel, and think we need or deserve.

My friend lost considerable weight by applying this Scripture: *Whether you **eat or drink**, or whatever you do, do all **to the glory of God*** (1 Cor. 10:31). Each meal, she reminded that junk food didn't let her glorify the Father with her body. She saw self-denial of unhealthy foods as her way of taking up her cross daily and following Jesus (Lk. 9:23). Dying to self means to deny self, which she did. When asked how she lost so much weight, she replied, *"By glorifying the LORD."*

We give the Lord glory because He is perfect in holiness and love. God cannot not love, for love defines who God is. He can be no other way. He can do only good. His mercy is holy mercy. All His attributes pure. He is fire, and His fire is holy fire used for helping men be saved. He is light, and no darkness is in Him. His laws are holy justice, and His name holy. He is the absolute standard for all that's good and right, and His faithfulness is inseparable from His holy Covenants.

Jesus created our world out of nothing in order to display the Father's glory so all inhabitants can declare His greatness and display His love and goodness to others. He does this so we want to be saved and spend eternity with Him as much as He wants to spend it with us (2 Pe. 3:9). Because He offers us a way to be saved without us having to pay the debt of our sins, it earns Him the right of having first place in our lives and receiving all praise. The Father is glorified when we are baptized and accept Jesus as our Savior, give credit to Him for our achievements and right decisions, and when we help others be saved.

Yet, how often we fail to depend on Him before making decisions. We ignore that He is the source of our skills, resources, energy, our very existence. I pray for churches who spend part of their worship service praising each other's achievements without mentioning who blessed them with the ability. No wonder so few people realize their need of the Lord and think themselves wise and talented enough without Him. If they don't learn at home or worship that they live totally dependent on Him for all they do and have, where will they?

Jesus is the true vine, and our Holy Father is the gardener. Only by being in Jesus are we able to bear fruit that has heavenly value. If we bear good fruit, the Father prunes us so we can do even more, but if we refuse to produce any fruit, the Father cuts off every barren branch. (Jn. 15:1-4). If we take credit for our fruitful achievements, we have stolen from the Lord because righteousness comes through Jesus Christ to the glory and praise of God (Phil 1:9-11). We have no righteousness of our own.

As Paul taught the Ephesians, *we are God's workmanship, created in Christ Jesus to do good **works, which God prepared in advance for us to do*** (Eph. 2:8-10 my emphasis). Whatever we achieve, it is because as He was creating us, He graced us with the ability and resources.

However, many times, how we choose to be is more important than what we do because our state of being may over shadow our tasks. For example, if my husband is frustrated with repairing something and snaps at my interruption, I'm left with response choices. I can react to him based on how his words leave me feeling, or I can remember how God wants me to be. However, when I think I have been treated rudely I tend to want to immediately seeking self-protection by counter attacking him. Yet, he may have had no intention of sounding curt, and I have misinterpreted his tone. His tone may have nothing to do with me at all. But it's easier to believe I am correct, not check the interpretation I assigned to him, and respond according to what I think he meant. Only I know that answering by how I feel is using the excuse, *"He did it first,"* and that reason didn't excuse Adam either.

I can attempt to self-protect by reacting by how I feel and bring up a long list of his faults, but this adds another sin to my account, not his. *Starting a quarrel is like breaching a dam; so, drop the matter before a dispute breaks out* (Prov. 17:14). Or, I can do something special for him, as Jesus so often modeled. I might make his favorite cookies, and as I mix the ingredients, pray about Satan's temptation to have me to react rudely. I can serve him warm cookies and milk and if he says that I didn't have to do that, I can honestly say, *"Of course, I did. Making something you like is a way I demonstrate my love for you and for Jesus, even when I'm not sure how I should interpret the tone of your voice,"* as I kiss his cheek and walk away.

Obeying God's Word always reaps positive results: *Do not* **repay** *evil with evil or insult with insult, but* **with blessings,** *because to this you were called* ***so that*** ***you may inherit a blessing*** (1 Pe. 3:9 my emphasis). Just think, **we receive a blessing for responding to an insult in a polite way, instead of reacting as we feel.** We have choices of either working for God's blessing or adding another sin to our name. How God expects us to be has no dependence on how another treats us. It's how we are supposed to be as we serve the Lord so our interactions bring glory to the Father -- no matter if another's words or behaviors are unkind.

We get no credit (reward) in heaven if our good deeds aren't done because we love the Lord. I now realize how true this is. We read of atheists who make outstanding contributions in today's world, but compared to eternity, their works count nothing for salvation. To ignore God, as we do good for others, disrespects our Father giving His only Son to save us and denies the Holy Spirit of developing in us the talents that let us accomplish all we do. Our love and talents that we carry around in *our jars of clay* have their source only in Him (2 Cor. 4:7). We are to use our skills to bear fruit that glorifies our Holy Father, not shine the spotlight on ourselves.

We get no credit (reward) in heaven if our good deeds aren't done because we love the Lord

In the past, I have no idea how many meals I have taken to ill friends. Only I did it because I loved the friends, not to honor the Lord. For months, I sewed little girl dresses for a poor family because our church was helping them. I received praise for how nice the dresses were, but nothing from the Lord. I didn't even think about Him as I sewed. I have no idea how many times I trudged up and down streets asking for donations for a worthwhile charity and was thrilled to turn in so much money and receive attention. Others were helped, but I gained nothing in heaven. As God's Word says, *"I had my reward in full,"* by receiving other's praise (Mt. 6:5; Lk. 6:24). I didn't know a man is tested by the praise he receives (Prov. 27:21). *It is not honorable to seek one's own honor* (Prov.25:27).

God knows the motives in our hearts. He knows the reasons we do good things for others. For years, I didn't understand that my skills, money, and time should honor the Father, and that afterwards, I should thank Him for having given me the ability to accomplish such tasks. Because all my prior good works were done for wrong reasons, they will be burned away on Judgment Day (1 Cor. 3:13). I will not be rewarded as I could have been if I had only understood years earlier that all I say and do are to glorify the Father.

Today, I realize it is only because of Him that I knew how to cook and had money to buy foods to prepare. It was with His blessing that I had a sewing machine and knew how to sew. It was to His credit that I wasn't too shy to ask others to donate to a worthwhile charity. And each time, I thanked Him for nothing. Yes, others were helped, but according to Matthew, I gain no heavenly reward for those years of work. *Be careful not to do your acts of righteousness before men to be seen by them. If you do, you will have* no *reward from your Father in heaven* (Mt. 6:2). If we aren't working to bring glory to the Father then all time and energy is as Solomon, the wisest of men, called the time in his life when he was without the Lord: *"Meaningless! Meaningless!"* (Ecc. 12:8). And it is the same in a career where we work or attend school. Are your daily tasks and how you are as you do them meant to put the Father first and have others honor Him?

While Paul is noted for complimenting others, it was for how such people helped so others could be saved, not for their own individual accomplishments. In fact, when Ananias and Sapphira wanted praise for donating money to the Lord's work and exaggerated the amount, God immediately struck them dead (Ac. 5:1-11). God let King Herod be eaten by worms when he failed to tell the people not to call him god (Ac. 12:21-

23). The Father refuses to let others share glory that's rightfully His.

We are not saved by our works. We are saved by faith in Jesus and God's grace. God sent His Son to seal us for the day of redemption (2 Cor. 1:22; Eph 4:30). Our eternity is secure. Works determine the rewards we receive in heaven. Helping others proves the depth of our faith and appreciation for His grace. But we are saved because of Christ's work, not ours.

Our life should be about displaying the Father's glory by being helpful, generous, honest, and having a positive attitude as we help others. *Anyone who knows the good he ought to do and doesn't do it, sins* (Js. 4:17). We ensure others know we do helpful things because the Father gives us the skills and resources to do them. *Let your light so shine before men that they may* **see your good works and give glory to your Father** *in heaven* (Mt. 5:16 my emphasis). Even Jesus said, *"I seek not my own glory, but the glory of Him who sent me"* (Jn. 8:50).

The day we stop lying to ourselves about all we think we do on our own and realize how deeply we depend on our Holy Father is the day we give the Father due glory and stop bragging about ourselves. The day we honestly admit our weaknesses is the day we welcome being dependent on Him and feel comfortable with it. We will acknowledge it is our Father working in us, with us, and for us, and we can't thank Him enough.

We glorify the Father by praying about everything – before we do it. We seek His guidance, trust He's giving it, and patiently await His response. We don't ask and go about things as we had already decided, but pray about our concern and genuinely believe what we decide after our prayers is because He planned it. We admit that He gave us the strength to study for an exam and had us studying the correct material so we passed. We praise Him for the person who gives us a suggestion we had not considered, believing He put the person in our face. When our child returns to the Lord, or we are healed of an illness, or we find a new job, it is our Father's glory shining through our lives, and we thank Him. Faith is trust that is proven with actions of obedience. We thank and praise Him for our care so others see all He does for us, so they too want to know Him. When we credit our Father and thank Him, He is glorified, and He blesses us with more opportunities. When we make mistakes, we ask our Father to take charge and work things for our good. He's the One who sees all options and has the power to change things for our good, – and then we use His plan to bring Him the glory.

When we credit our Father and thank Him, He is glorified, and He blesses us with more opportunities

We do the work, our Father gets the praise, and we thank Him for giving us the ability to accomplish the task. Then He gives us brownie points in His Book of Life. *The Son of Man is* *going to come in His Father's glory with His angels, and then He will **reward each person according to what he has done*** (Mt. 16:27). We will be rewarded in heaven for our good works done here on earth - provided we give the glorify to the Father.

While they are young, we need to teach our children that their abilities and talents depend on the Father. We encourage them to develop the skills the Father gives them: to pursue things they love doing and can spend hours so engrossed doing they lose track of time. They should go after it with all their heart - and use that talent to help others. Such abilities are their own personal, individual gift from the Father. *"Each one should use whatever gift he has received to serve others, faithfully administering God's grace in its various forms"* (1 Pe. 4: 10). We help them credit our Father for their ability to do it. *"If anyone serves, he should do it with the **strength God provides, so that in all things God may be praised through Jesus Christ"*** (v.11 my emphasis). It's not us who are to be praised and not our children.

God claims the children we bring into the world belong to Him (Eze. 16:20) and He calls them *'My children'* (v. 21). It's our role to ensure they know they belong to Him. When they make Him the leader of their lives, they bring Him great glory.

TESTED vs TEMPTED

Becoming a Christian often requires that we move beyond our comfort level, as Abraham did when asked to sacrifice his son. God will test us with trials, many we could not have foreseen. He will put us in the fiery furnace of affliction multiple times (Isa. 48:10-11), to meet us in our place of greatest need. He does this to strengthen our faith, improve our character, and make us conscious of the ways we sin so we will repent. This purifies our hearts and souls and strengthens our relationship with Him. At the same time, Satan attacks and tempts us to rebel and disobey the Lord. Jesus strengthens our faith to bond a tighter relationship with Him. Satan works to have us miss heaven and suffer with him and his evil spirits in hell. Satan does this because he knows losing our salvation hurts the Lord. Living the Christian life is to live in the midst of a spiritual war, but Jesus is always in the midst to support us. We only have to ask for His help.

If we prove too slow in practicing self-denial of things that hinder our relationship with Jesus Christ, or if we attempt to ignore or justify behaviors we need to correct, the Lord with the Holy Spirit's help will force us to *clean up our act*. He does this because He longs for a deeper, restored relationship (Isa.

5:1; 66:13-14; Mt. 23:37; Joel 2: 12-13). We have stubborn wills that need serious transformation to become like Christ and return His love (Ro. 8:28-30). Our natural inclination is not to submit to God but to seek our own glory and resist turning to Jesus' call to become like little children who depend fully on Him. With baptism, we are given the Holy Spirit to help us do this (Ro. 8:7-9). There is no part of life we have to handle alone.

Once we wear Christ's name as Christian, Jesus comes and meets us where we are, but because He loves us, He is not willing to let us remain as we are. He insists that we grow spiritually. He disciplines us with spiritual tests that produce obedience and have us becoming more like Him. For this, we need our hearts changed and a desire for eternity planted deep within our souls. Our tests are a work of His grace.

The Bible is filled with ways God tested people. For example, God sent the Israelites bread from heaven to test them. He said to Moses, *"I will rain down bread. Gather enough for that day. In this way I will **test them and see whether they will follow my instructions**"* (Ex. 16:4). Moses told the people, *"Do not be afraid. God has come to **test you, so that the fear of God will be with you to keep you from sinning**"* (Ex. 20:20). Moses explained, "He gave you manna to eat in the desert, something your fathers had never known, **to humble and to test you so that in the end it might go well with you**" (Dt.

230

8:16). Since creation, God's instructions have always been for the benefit of His people's salvation, and He ensured they knew it.

God's instructions have always been for the benefit of people's salvation

We need to remember that God is leading this test, not us, which means we can succeed. He sees our problems, our deepest heartaches, and emotional drains. This has Him wanting to transform our hearts so we grow in Him and become more loving with fewer hurts. We have to trust Him and be willing to grow (Ro. 12:1-2).

Many of Jesus' tests seriously disrupt our daily routines, and force us to examine our spiritual condition. We must decide if we are going to remain faithful or be disobedient. He refuses to let us remain in a lukewarm, half-in half-out condition (Rev. 3:15-16; Tit.1:16; Mt. 12:30). He wants us to realize we are choosing either life with Him or life in the lake of fire with Satan. Lukewarmness is dangerous. It produces a pretense of faith that has people thinking they are acceptable with the Lord, but actually doing little that's right and missing heaven.

After accepting Jesus as our Lord and Savior with baptism, we live saved forever unless we choose to deny Him, abandon our faith, and become so entangled in sin that our heart hardens to the point of no return (1 Cor. 11:30; Prov. 28:14; Ro. 2:5). But know, every Christian wrestles daily with sin. Even Paul complained that he failed to do what he wanted and did what he hated. It was sin living in him. He sinned against his will that wanted to follow the Lord perfectly. (Ro. 7:15-20). Scripture is clear that we need to frequently examine the condition of our hearts to ensure we are right with the Lord (2 Cor.13:5). How dreadful to believe that what we do wrong is not a big deal, and have our conscious become so calloused that what we call acceptable is actually sinful. It's why Jesus continually taught men to repent. When we choose to sin, we put a barrier between us and the Lord, and it's up to us to ask God to remove it. Sadly, many want to run from the Lord and face a dreadful eternity, rather than repent and change. It is often at this point that God brings tests to force us to admit our wrongs, confess and change. He works continually to save us.

Some of our trials create minor disruptions or embarrassment while others require more serious challenges to grab our attention. A minor test that served as a reminder of what Philip should have known, was when Jesus recognized the need to feed a large crowd. He asked Philip, *"Where shall we buy bread for these people to eat?"* He asked this **only to test him**, *for He already had in mind what He was going to* *do"* (Jn. 6:5-6 my emphasis). Philip had forgotten to depend on Jesus' miraculous ability, but after this embarrassing test, I doubt Philip forgot again.

If a small test fails to awake us to our need to cleanse our heart's, Jesus will force us to face more serious, even severe trials. If we attempt to ignore His test, He appears to wait and give us time to change. If we don't, we better prepare for the next challenge, because each following test becomes more difficult to bear. With each one, He makes us well aware of worsened discomfort, pain, and misery. Each exam is based on what is required to wake us to our need to reexamine our standing with Him (2 Cor. 13:5-7). The more stubborn and rebellious we remain, the more fire of distress and pain there is in the next test. However, if we become aware of Jesus' test and quickly self-evaluate, confess, and change, the challenge soon ends, and we enjoy a time of peace until we again stray or need our faith strengthened. The beneficial part is that with change comes spiritual cleansing, a deepened faith, and more confidence of heaven.

Every test God sends is to remove remaining sin in our lives and to have us rely more completely on Him. For example, a minor test might be by a two-year-old who won't stop screaming "No" at our every request. God stands ready to relieve our stress and show us how to stop such misbehavior, provided we repent of our times of losing control. A more serous test might be facing an unbearable supervisor. God will show us how to gain his fellowship, provided we confess our own wrongs in the struggle. If we don't repent, we are likely to experience added problems with others who like and appreciate the supervisor until things become so unbearable. we must quit or be fired. If we have alienated ourself from the Lord for too long, a severe, harsh test might be required and us face something very serious, like a tragic accident. If we admit how the sinful things we did contributed, we will heal faster. But if we revert back and continue in willful sins, our health will continue to worsen with each succeeding trial -- until we finally submit and repent. However, if after repeated tests, we continue to refuse to repent, God will let us go to pursue our sinful ways and spend eternity in hell. Remember He gave Cain three chances to change. When Cain failed, God let him go to pursue his own way and face eternal damnation. Conversely, if we do an honest self-evaluation, admit sins in our lives, and seek His forgiveness, the Lord responds with healing. He wants to work every situation for our spiritual good (Ro. 8:28).

Even the godliest people sin and need to seek forgiveness. Realizing a need to change proves we want to love the Lord and be loved by Him. However, if we had to confess every sin, none of us would make heaven. If we sin, and don't realize it or forget it and die, we still stand in His righteous grace. Believers trying to remain faithful rely on Jesus' righteousness and remain heaven bound (Php. 3:9-11). As long as we are striving to walk in His Light, we have fellowship with one another, and the **blood of Jesus purifies us from all sin** (1 Jn. 1:7 my emphasis). Still, we seek forgiveness because of how confession strengthens our faith, cleanses our consciences, and helps transform us into the image of Christ so we represent Him well in our daily lives. Every time we repent, Jesus speaks to His Father in our defense (Heb. 7;25; 1 Jn. 2:1). With repentance and Jesus' defense, we can't lose.

Even the godliest people sin and need to seek forgiveness

Salvation is based on our faith in Christ and God's grace (Ro. 10: 9-10 my emphasis). Remember, with baptism, Jesus sent us the Holy Spirit that sealed His promise of our redemption (2 Cor. 1:22; Eph. 4:30). We are saved by grace, not by works we do. We won't miss heaven if we have no works that God considers of eternal value so long as we have faith and trust in Jesus and are striving to live as He commands (1 Cor. 3:11-15). However, good deeds prove our faith. The stronger our faith, and the more we love Jesus for dying for us, the more we want to do things to helps others. It's why James says we show our faith by what we do, and a faith not accompanied by actions (good deeds) is dead (Js. 2:17, 26). Since works determine our heavenly rewards, why would anyone not want to help others, knowing it means they will enjoy heaven even more?

Because God loves us, even as we sin, He disciplines us (Ro. 5:8). That does not mean we won't face consequences or suffer pain of a forgiven sin. A thief may receive the Lord's forgiveness but still be required to go to prison. None of us who wear Christ's name are sinless. However, we should examine our lives and find that our thoughts and actions reflect more holiness and less wrongdoing today than when we were first saved. Jesus leads this work through the Holy Spirit to transform us into His likeness (2 Cor. 3:17-18).

Once we respond with humble repentance, He brings us mercy and comfort and gives us work to do for Him. For example, Jesus forewarned Peter to prepare for Satan's temptation. Instead of Jesus stopping Satan's attack of Peter, He told Peter that He was praying for his faith not to fail and for him to strengthen his brothers. Peter failed and later was restored by the Lord. Afterwards, Peter became one of Jesus' boldest teachers (Lk. 22:31-32).

Once we accept that God is in control of our difficult, trying situations, we can be assured that things will end for our good. His grace is sufficient for us, and His power is being proven perfect during our times of weakness (2 Cor. 12:9). Paul asked the Lord three times to remove his thorn in the flesh because he recognized Satan could use it to tempt him. Instead, of healing Paul, Jesus told him, *"My grace is sufficient for you, for my power is made perfect in weakness* (2 Cor.12:9). Later, Paul explained, *"For Christ's sake, I delight in weaknesses like insults, hardships, persecutions, and in difficulties. For when I am weak, then I am strong."* Paul realized his strength came from being totally dependent on the Lord's care of him. This let Paul be content no matter the trial he faced or the temptation Satan brought. He learned that God would ensure his troubles resulted in positive outcomes (Ro. 8:28).

We will all face tests. How we handle them is our choice. We can accept them, spend added time in His Word, pray more, and learn to more quickly acknowledge any unforgiven sin. If we do, we are assured we will end each one with added confidence that we are heaven bound. *We must learn to endure hardship as discipline, for God is treating you as sons. **Submit** to the Father of our spirits **and live!*** (Heb. 12: 7,9). His tests help remove sin from our lives and make us fit for heaven.

However, if we continually refuse to admit any sins, we risk our heart hardening beyond the Holy Spirit's reach, and losing our heavenly reward. Daniel was told, *"Many will be purified, made spotless and refined, but the wicked will continue to* be wicked. *None of the wicked will understand, but* **those who are wise will understand**" *(12:10)*. The wise practice ongoing repentance.

In what areas of your life do you need deepest healing? What areas are you experiencing the most emotional, physical, financial, or spiritual pain? Can you recognize His testing? You can respond, have your heart and mind transformed, and be healed. The choice is yours.

Meanwhile, Satan attacks believers to have them turn away from the Lord and face eternal damnation. Once we are baptized, Satan's assaults begin. Satan can ignore hardened unbelievers because they already belong to him. If we respond to Satan's temptation, we are choosing to be a servant to Satan and he uses us as his pawns for hurting God. The more people Satan can have challenge God's commands or walk away from the Lord, the happier he is. For that means he has wrecked God's desire for *all to be saved and come to a knowledge of the truth* (1 Ti. 2:4). We must remember that he can appear as an angel of light (2 Cor. 11:13-15), but even then, he is a nothing compared to God.

When we are suffering, we want to blame someone or find an explanation, and some blame God. We forget that God doesn't answer to us, and if He did answer our why questions, we probably would not understand. God sees us in relation to eternity, a view we can't see or grasp. We forget that when He created mankind, pain and death were not part of His plan. It was caused by man's misuse of free will. Suffering is a result of men responding to Satan's temptations, and it has worked since the time of Adam and Eve.

We may be tempted by Satan, as Job was, but remember that Job's temptations were still under God's sovereign control. God sets limits on how far Satan can push us (2 Cor. 4:8-9), and promises that we will not be tempted beyond what we can bear (1 Cor. 10:13). God allowed Job such a severe temptation because of how good Job was and how he strove to live right. *Job was blameless and upright; he feared God and shunned evil* (Job 1:1). Just as God saw Job as righteous, He sees baptized believers the same way, not because of how they are, but because of the work Jesus did for them on the cross. Still, there was another lesson Job needed to learn, and God used Satan's temptation to teach him. God used what Satan meant as evil to strengthen Job spiritually.

While Jesus intercedes for us with the Father, Satan, the accuser, points out our sins, as he did with Job by using men, who were supposed to be Job's friends, to criticize him (Job 1:6-12). Because of Satan, Job lost all his children, his health was ruined, and his wife asked him to deny God. Job asked God 16 times to tell him why such bad things were happening.

Instead of answering Job's questions, God showed Job how severely inferior in every way he was when compared to God, and how he could fully trust God's loving strength to care for him. Once Job realized the magnitude of God's great love and power, Job no longer needed to know why such things happened. Job knew that God knew the reasons, and with his stronger, trusting faith, Job knew God would use His loving power to care for his every need. Job's trusting relationship with God was now genuine, and God blessed him with more of everything that Satan had taken from him.

Neither Satan nor his demons can tempt or afflict us beyond what God allows. Because all trials work toward God's perfect purpose of making us pure enough to become part of His heavenly family, God keeps a firm limit on Satan. During the most trying of Satan's temptations, when we prove faithful, we find God ultimately working the situation for our eternal good with things better than before (Ro. 8:28). However, it rarely seems that way while in the midst of a stressful situation until we remember that to be in the midst refers to Jesus' presence. During a test that's by Jesus or amid a temptation by Satan, we are never abandoned by Jesus. He's in the midst of our test waiting for our request seeking His help.

God protects us so we can bear his tests. If we lose our job, face a serious illness, or our children reject us, He is with us showing us ways to endure. But His care only lasts as long or remains as strong as we allow. The more honestly, we admit how our sinful desires contributed, the more He can continue helping. We can fight His testing and react in sinful ways, but if we realize it is His doing and immediately repent, we will come through the trial with blessings beyond what we may have lost. Just as Job finally did.

Job acknowledged believing that we face continual spiritual tests from God. Job asked, *"What is man that you make so much of him, that **you give him so much attention**, that you examine him every morning and **test him every moment?"** (Job 7:17-18). Job recognized that his test proved how deeply he was loved by the Lord. If God didn't love us, He would have abandoned us long ago. Instead, He keeps making us fit to live with Him for eternity, as He did Job: *"In all this, Job did not sin with his lips"* (2:10).

Job recognized that his test proved how deeply he was loved by the Lord

We need to exit our trials so cleansed of sin and trusting of the Lord that we ask of God what David asked: *Though you probe my heart and examine me at night, though you **test me, you will find nothing***; I have resolved that my mouth will not sin (Ps.

17:3). Test me, O LORD, and try me, examine my heart and my mind (Ps. 26:2). David wanted to prove his loyalty. God wants the same from each of us today. . . so He finds less need to test us. The more we depend on Him, confess our sins, change, and focus on helping others know Him, the fewer and shorter tests we are required to face.

Paul reminds that we should not be trying to please men but God, *who tests our hearts* (1 Th. 2:4). God wants to ensure that the motives in our hearts are focused on remaining faithful. James teaches, *"Count it all joy, my brothers, when you meet trials of various kinds, for you know that **the testing of your faith produces steadfastness**. And let steadfastness have its full effect, that you may be perfect and complete, **lacking in nothing**. When we remain strong in the Lord, as we are being tested, we receive a spiritual reward"* (Js. 1:1-4 my emphasis). Blessed is the man who remains steadfast under trial, for when he has stood the test, he will receive the crown of life, which God has promised to those who love Him. And when our heart is right, others recognize it by how we behave and what we say.

Once we are enjoying heaven, we will thank the Lord for testing us, because without such trials, we might not be here. As Paul said, *"I consider that the present sufferings are not worth comparing with the glory that will be revealed to us"* (Ro. 8:18).

While you may have to suffer grief in all kinds of trials, they have come so your faith, though tested by fire, may be proved genuine and may result in praise, glory, and honor when Jesus Christ is revealed. . . **you are receiving the goal of your faith, the salvation of your souls** (1 Pe. 1:3-9 my emphasis). He tests us to ensure we join His heavenly family. One who wants to spend eternity with the Lord does not argue or ignore the Lord's tests, but happily repents of his sins and thanks Him. *You, O God tested us. . . you refined us like silver. . . laid burdens on our back. . . we went through fire and water, but you brought us to a place of abundance* (Ps. 66:10-12).

Currently, what is your biggest struggle? Financial? Health? Issues with your children? Be as honest as you can, and admit how you have sinned with your job or care of your money. Or how have you sinned in a lack of care for your spiritual health? Or in what ways would your children say you have sinned that's left them hurt? Confess your sin to God, commit to change, and ask Him to help you correct your life. You will be like Job and David and realize you were tested because God loves you and wants your life pure enough so you can enjoy heaven with Him. It works that way every time. He promises.

HOW OFTEN WE SIN

After studying lessons on the necessity of baptism, and how our pledge to keep a clean conscience binds us to God's New Covenant promises, my Bible teacher said we needed to study how frequently, as baptized believers, we contaminate our hearts with sin. He insisted we all sin daily, and some days multiple times. He reminded that Paul explained that **all** sin and fall short of the glory of God (Ro. 3:23). What makes Christians different from other sinners is they feel guilt for their sins, as the Holy Spirit presses them to change. Such was the prodigal son story in Luke. After his sins left him penniless and hungry, He was led to go home, or as Scripture says, *'when he came to his senses,'* he got up and went home to openly confess, *"Father, I have sinned against heaven and against you. I am no longer worthy to be called your son"* (Lk. 15:18-19). When the guilt of sin affects our hearts, we know we won't rest until we go to the Lord and repent. Just like the the prodigal son's father did, when God sees we are prepared to change, He races to welcome us back home.

Paul stressed that being baptized washed away all sins we had previously committed and if we remain faithful to the end of our days, we are guaranteed heaven (Mt. 24:13; Col. 1:23;

Jas. 1:22-24). Repentance of our ongoing sins lets the Lord keep our hearts and consciences pure as He forgives and remembers our sins no more.

The teacher stressed how powerful the word **if** is and questioned, *"If we continue to sin without loving the Lord enough to repent of our sins, will we still be heaven-bound?"* He reminded how Jesus' dying and becoming our Holy Priest offers us freedom to go directly to our Holy Father to repent in prayer and lets Him forgive our every wrong. Only first, we must admit our sins. We won't repent of sins we excuse or ignore. He emphasized that no matter our type of wrongdoing we will all answer to God for sinful words and actions.

The teacher reminded what God said after Adam and Eve ate the forbidden fruit: *"The man has now become like one of us, knowing good and evil"* (Ge. 3:22). Adam's and Eve's guilt let them know they had done something so wrong they wanted to hide (Ge. 3:10). They learned, as we need to realize today, that no sins are ever hidden from God, especially those of baptized believers. With baptism, the Holy Spirit comes to live within our hearts and is continually in our hearts and thoughts observing all we do.

The teacher asked that during the coming week we begin each day reading Hebrews 4: 12-13. *For **the word** of God **is living and active**. Sharper than any double-edged sword, **it*** *penetrates even to dividing soul and spirt, joints and marrow; it judges the thoughts and attitudes of the heart. Nothing in all creation is hidden from God's sight. Everything is uncovered and laid bare before the eyes of Him to whom we must give an account.* Go back and read only the emphasized words several times.

Our teacher stressed that we think of God as being passive and far away, not that the Holy Spirit lives within our hearts. We forget that every time we sin, we do so in His presence. We cannot hide from Him. If we steal something, God the Holy Spirit is inside us trying to have us do what's right. As we sneak from the store, He pressures us to return what we took or pay for it. The teacher said as parents we should emphasize to our teens if they have sex in the back seat of a car, they are doing so with the Holy Spirit beside them. We need to teach that no matter our sin, the Holy Spirit is actively assessing us, be it sexual, lying, gossiping, or whatever, He is inside us, nudging us to stop and do what's right by God's moral and ethical law.

Our teacher insisted that because God's laws are in believer's hearts, we intuitively know when we sin. We are made in God's image, and when we sin, we tarnish our likeness. We were created to model the glory of God's goodness to others (Ro. 11:22; Isa. 43:7). Every sin we commit has us violating God's moral commands, and He holds us accountable for breaking our baptismal pledge to keep a clean heart. If we don't immediately realize our wrong, the Holy Spirit presses us to ensure we can no longer ignore it.

Sin is anything that violates God's law. Even if our sins harm no other, which is rare, our every wrong, hurts our Savior. Remember Jesus said when we sin, we are telling him, **I *despise Your word, I hate You, I detest Your Covenant, hate You testifying that I do evil and hate Your Light for exposing my sin*"** (2 Sam. 12:9-10; Jn. 7:7, 15:18 my emphasis). Ouch!

The Bible teacher challenged our class to pause and honestly admit and prayerfully confess how we sinned each day during the coming week. I accepted the challenge, arrogantly thinking he was surely mistaken about it being daily.

I just didn't think I sinned every day. Some days, yes. Many days, yes, but every day sounded too often, especially since I was home alone most of each day. My husband left very early for work, sometimes before I even woke, and he didn't return home until about 6:00 pm. He and I rarely had a spat. Overall, our relationship was very good, and he is a kind, generous man. So, if I was going to sin, it would likely be while I was home alone, and I just didn't know how I could do that.

I spent each day developing seminars to present to the general public who paid to attend. I was currently writing one I called Handling Anger. When I was about half finished, I remembered something I should have added several pages earlier. As I was scrolling back, the telephone rang.

At that time, sales calls were made by a live person, unlike today's robocalls. The man on the phone kept pushing and pressing, even to the point of angrily arguing after I thanked him several times and said I had no interest. Finally, I could tolerate his hostile aggressiveness no longer. I rudely told him so, and slammed down the receiver.

That evening being rude to the caller was my sin to confess. I could have just as easily been polite and hung up, but I had let my frustration make me want to hurt him as much as he had annoyed me. Only at the time, I didn't admit I wanted to hurt him. I was too focused on his arrogant style and bad-mannered approach, not myself and what I had done wrong.

Isn't that how we immediately handle hurt feelings and annoyances? We let our negative emotions focus our thoughts on the other person, not on what we have done wrong or what we could have done differently to avoid the situation escalating. From my own experience and years of counseling others, I believe, **"Focusing on others' wrongs, instead of our**

own, is a major reason why we don't realize how often we sin." It is easier to point out others wrongs, than be honest about our own spiritual deficits. This lets Satan win again, like he did when Adam blamed Eve.

It is easier to point out others' wrongs, than be honest about our own spiritual deficits

Finally, the Holy Spirit forced me to face the truth about myself. He wouldn't let me ignore my part of the phone call. I had to admit what a hypocrite I had been thinking I could tell others how to handle anger when I had just blown it this badly. I confessed the sins of rudeness and my current hypocrisy and decided my phone call was a good example to use in programs.

The following day, I committed to being kind no matter what type of calls I might receive. I was determined not to sin. Midmorning, I realized I needed paper and decided to go to the office store. I remembered my commitment. I decided that no matter what a clerk or another customer might say, I would be polite.

As I approached a four-way stop, I arrived at the same time as an approaching car. I smiled and waved for him to go first. I mentally patted myself on the back thinking this was a good start in kindness. Then as I was about to go, a car was pulling to the intersection. As I began to move, this driver ran the stop sign and turned right which had us going in the same direction. To avoid him hitting my car's passenger side, I ran completely off the other side of the road. I sat trembling on the shoulder of the road, facing on-coming traffic.

My immediate thought was, *"I hope you get a ticket for driving so carelessly."* Then I recalled my commitment and calmed. I began a discussion inside my thoughts: *"Who am I to wish something bad on another? That's not my place. I don't know his reason."* God judges people's reasons, not me. My thoughts quickly shifted to why the driver may have ignored the stop sign. *"Perhaps, he was coming from the hospital where his child lay dying. Or, maybe, he had just been served divorce papers. Or, he could have just been thinking about something other than driving, as we all do at times, and simply failed to notice the stop sign. Or maybe, he was just a rude person, as I had been yesterday on the phone."* I knew the sin I had to confess, only I didn't wait until evening.

God judges people's reasons, not me

I have to admit that I sinned every day that week. My wise Bible teacher was correct. I sinned daily, and some sins were worse than I chose to share here. No wonder the Holy Spirit guided Paul to warn us. This assignment helped me appreciate that Jesus intercedes on our behalf by speaking with the Father when we confess a sin (Heb. 7:25; 1 Jn. 2:1), and it let me know how busy He must stay.

The wages of sin is death. Because we are sinners, and because God so often honors us with grace, we forget the evilness of our own sin. Instead of wondering why God killed idol worshippers, we should be asking, "Why doesn't He kill us all?" The part that should shock us is when we have periods of straying from Him, He always welcomes us back.

How we tend to focus exclusively on the first part of 1 Peter 3:21 that says: *"water symbolizes baptism that now saves you. . ."* while ignoring the remainder of the Scripture that says **baptism is** *"our pledge of a good conscience toward God."* Baptism is our vow, our commitment. It is our promise to do good deeds that help others because we love the Lord and to keep our conscience clean of sin. We can only do that by admitting and repenting of our sins so we receive God's promise to remember them no more. To love Jesus is to want to please Him (Jn. 14:15), and prayers of repentance, bond us to Him.

Ecclesiastes (5:4-5) cautions: *"When you make a vow to God, do not delay in fulfilling it. He has no pleasure in fools; fulfill your vow. It is better not to vow than to make a vow and not fulfill it"* (5:4-5). In Psalm it asks: *How can I repay the Lord for all His goodness to me?* Then answers: *I will fulfill my vows to the Lord (116:12).*

Obviously, we can overlook our sins and dirty our conscience so badly that we ignore how filthy our hearts have become. But with repentance, God forgives. The more we confess, the more we become conscious of what's right and what's wrong and learn to make better on-going decisions on the spot. It's part of putting off the old man and putting on a new born-again man with renewed knowledge of Christ's expectations (Col. 3:9-10).

After my trial week of admitting daily sins, I knew my goal had to become one of confessing and repenting immediately when I realize a wrong. I learned it's important because the more sins I confess, the more I realize how good the Father's forgiving grace is and how desperately I needed Jesus to redeem me from the debt my numerous sins left me owing Him. When we regret our sins, confess, and commit to change, we become as pure and cleansed as the day we were baptized. And Jesus taught it is the pure in heart who will see God (Mt. 5:8). What a blessing forgiveness and the Father's forgetting them is.

When we regret our sins, confess, and commit to change, we become as pure and cleansed as the day we were baptized

When we realize that we genuinely deserve hell, the more we love the Lord for His dying for us. Who else would die for you or me while we are amid our very worst wrongs? People would rather punish us or use us as gossip, but not the Lord. He still wants to love us and spend eternity with us.

When we fail to do what's right, our guilty conscience warns us of wrongdoing, and the Holy Spirit nudges us to change so we are again right with the Lord. We can have the will to self-correct our sinful behaviors, repent, and do as God asks. A heart that is soft and pliable restores full fellowship with the Lord, just as it did with King David after his sins.

When we repent, we are to have faith that God forgives and **purifies us from all unrighteousness** (1 Jn. 1:9 my emphasis). Once we repent, we have no need to mention the same sin again. We need to make things right with another we have hurt so we can release any guilt that remains, but God forgives and forgets the second we repent. We don't keep asking Him to forgive what He no longer recalls. If we keep mentioning the same sin, we are telling God that we think we have a higher moral standard than He does, and we don't believe His blood covers this particular sin, so His death was wasted on this wrong. We also are saying we don't believe Him when He says He remembers our sin no more. Ouch! That's calling God a liar.

Instead, we need to quickly interrupt such thoughts by asking the Lord to help us focus on other things until we can release such memories from our minds and hearts. We must guard against making our past sins our idol by giving them more attention and time than we use worshipping the Lord and studying His Word.

We address our prayers to our Holy Father, and close them with Jesus' name, our heavenly priest, who with the Holy Spirit intercedes for us. *Because Jesus lives forever, He has a permanent priesthood. Therefore, He is able to **save completely those who come to God through Him*** (Heb. 7:24 my emphasis).

Have you ever thought – seriously thought – about how our prayers grab Jesus' full attention, and He opens the realm of heaven where the Father reigns? When needed, Jesus and the Holy Spirit help word our prayers appropriately. Then angels pass our prayers with sweet smelling incense onto the Father. He listens to our appreciations and requests and sends answers back to earth that supply our current need (Rev. 8:3-5). What an amazing and blessed experience.

Some research shows we pray more often when we are deeply upset and troubled, and there's even a Scriptures that tells us how to pray at such times: *Do not be anxious about anything, but in everything by prayer and petition,* **with thanksgiving,** *present your request to God. And the peace of God, which transcends all understanding, will guard your hearts and your minds in Christ Jesus* (Phil 4:6-7 my emphasis). If we would do as this says, and first tell the Lord all we are thankful for, it would put many of our worries and desires in a proper perspective. If all we do or say is done in the name of the Lord Jesus, **giving thanks to God the Father through Him,** we realize how few requests we may actually need (Col. 3:17). Psalm teaches: *He who offers thank offerings honors Me and prepares the way so that I may show him the salvation of God* (50:23).

Closing our prayers in Jesus' name confirms we are coming to our Father, not of our own worth, but coming in Jesus' name because He is holy and because He sacrificed His blood to save us. Our obeying Jesus brings the Father glory. Because Jesus told His disciples, *"I will come back and take you to be with Me that you may also be where I AM* (Jn. 14;14), our prayer ending shows we appreciate having such a promise.

What joy we feel once we repent of a sin. What a relief to let go of guilt and know God has forgiven us. And what a blessing to know that to the Lord we look as clean and pure as new fallen snow.

POWER OF PRAYER

Keeping baptism's pledge is our Covenant obligation for receiving God's promises. *Water symbolizes* **baptism that now saves you**, *not the removal of dirt from our body but* **the pledge of a good conscience toward God** (1 Pe. 3:21 my emphasis). With baptism, we are making a promise to the Lord that we will strive to keep our conscience clean of wrongdoing by obeying His commands. That obviously requires training ourselves to identify sin, avoid doing wrong, repent when we sin, and do things that help others recognize the Lord's goodness. To live faithfully requires frequent prayers.

Jesus prayed often and stayed in close contact with His Father. He woke early to begin His day talking with His Father, and in the evenings going to the mountain to pray. At times, He prayed all night. He drew strength from His Father to fulfill His mission. His life showed prayer's importance, and it had the apostles asking Him to teach them to pray. Thus, we have the Lord's Prayer provide by Matthew and Luke, not so we can memorize it and repeat it verbatim, but so we understand prayer's purpose and importance.

John MacArthur, author of *Jesus: Pattern of Prayer*, studied the depth of the Lord's Prayer and offers valuable insight. He says: *Our Father who are in heaven*, shows a Father-child relationship; a family spirit, who adores a loving, generous Father. *Hallowed be Thy name*, displays a Deity-worshiper relationship, and requires us to have a reverent spirit. *Thy kingdom come*, reveals a Sovereign king with a subject and requires a loyal spirit. He's the King who can pardon the sinful debts we owe. *Thy will be done* is a Master-servant relationship and shows we are to have a submissive spirit because He's the Master who leads and protect us from temptation. It shows *His will* is our purpose to fulfill. *Give us our daily bread* is a benefactor--beneficiary relationship and proves our need to have a dependent spirit so that He provides our daily physical provisions. *Forgive us our debts* proves He's the Savior of sinners. This demands a penitent spirit so He can pardon our wrongs and give us mental and emotional relief of guilt. *Lead us not into temptation* is the relationship of a guide and pilgrim. It takes a humble spirit to allow another to lead us, but our reward for His leadership is knowing we live spiritually protected. *For Thine is the kingdom* offers us a confident spirit of our living in heaven. *The glory* shows an joyful spirit and *the power forever* is a triumphant spirit that proves us a winner.

The first four parts of the Lord's Prayer place the Father on His rightful, holy throne. Jesus was saying we should hold up the Father with the highest respect as we begin every prayer. When we put the Father on the altar He deserves, everything in our prayer and in our lives flows as it should. Christians' requests fall in the middle, where we are required to be for having daily needs provided, sins pardoned, and receiving His protection. The last three lines prove our lives depend on Him, and thanking Him exalts the Father in His deserved glory. The prayer shows we are completely surrounded by the Father's care. Seeking forgiveness is the only petition in the prayer that comes with a condition. We are to forgive, so we will be forgiven. God will help us stop thinking of hurtful, harmful situations if we continue to ask, and ultimately, we can let it go. We can do this when we remember the condition is for our own emotional and spiritual healing.

When we put the Father on the altar He deserves, everything in our prayer and in our life flows as it should

No greater prayer example of genuine repentance is there than how King David sought to cleanse his conscience of sin and purify his heart after his sexual sin with Bathsheba. According to the Law, they should have been killed. Likewise, David should have been killed for his sin of having her husband, Uriah, murdered. Instead, God forgave David because of how sincerely he repented. We have all been despicably evil. The more we realize it, the more God longs to forgive us – but first we must ask. We need to learn how to pray and ask as David did in Psalms (51). Examine David's prayer, and compare it with your own prayers. We must never miss God's forgiveness simply because we think we are so good that we have no need to repent, and therefore, fail to ask. Below is David's prayer. David's words are highlighted and followed by my personal interpretation of his intent.

Verse 1: ***Have mercy on me, O God, according to your unfailing love, according to your great compassion blot out my transgressions.*** David knew that his forgiveness required an act of grace that he didn't deserve. Before confessing his sin, David pled for God's compassion. He asked, "Address my sinful condition with Your tender, and undeserved grace. Because of God's great compassion David asked, "God, blot out my sin." He knew he didn't deserve forgiveness, but he knew God is merciful, and he needed His grace. Only because God loves us do our sins pain Him so deeply.

Verse 2: ***Wash away my iniquity and cleanse me from my sin.*** Blotting out David's current sin was not enough. He wanted deeper cleansing. He asked, "Wash me and ensure I am thoroughly cleansed, O God. Leave no sin of any kind in

me. Awake my conscience. Let me see every sin I have committed. Purify me." David is concerned with all the evilness he had committed against God, not just his recent sins. God hates even the sins that men consider tiny. David knew that only total truth with full exposure could set him free.

Verse 3: ***For I know my transgression, and my sin is always before me.*** David was saying, "I have committed many sins, and I am prepared to admit them all so I can be right with you O God. My sins are eating at my heart. I am repulsed at my behaviors. Guilt overwhelms me. I need You, O God, to release me mentally and emotionally so I am free to worship You again." David wanted to serve God as a true follower, not as a hypocrite. Deeper than his sinful desires was David's longing to do God's will. He knew the value of trusting the Lord and not trying to live life on his own.

Verse 4: ***Against you, you only, have I sinned, and done what is evil in your sight.*** David knew he had wronged Bathsheba and her husband, but ultimately every sin, including those against our fellow man, lie at the throne of God for His judgment. "Every sin is a sin against You, O God. I am guilty and offer no excuses for you have seen all my sins." He knew God would be fully justified in striking him dead, and only God's mercy would save him. He admitted being spiritually sick and in need of God's healing.

Verse 5: *Surely, I was sinful at birth, sinful from the time my mother conceived me.* David realized he had been disobedient since a child. Surely, he had rebelled against his parents and had done no better as an adult in being accountable to the Lord. "I confess how wrong I have been since a child and do no better now as an adult. I have lived in sin, instead of serving you. I am guilty, Lord." David wanted no sin hidden or forgotten so he could be certain he was purified. He knew God knows our unforgiven sins, no matter how many years ago they may have occurred.

Verse 6: *Surely you desire truth in the inner parts, you teach me wisdom in the inmost place.* David asked, "Cleanse my soul, my heart, and my conscience, and replace my wickedness with Your wisdom so I can truly change. I want to do what's right and do it for all the right reasons." He didn't just want his outward actions improved; he wanted the motives and reasons driving his behavior corrected.

Verse 7: *Cleanse me with hyssop, and I will be clean, wash me, and I will be whiter than snow.* David asks, "Use a hyssop branch to cover me with blood. Let my sin offering remove the sinful strain on my soul. But do more. Wash me again. Keep cleaning me until I am as white as a new fallen snow. Don't leave a speck of sin in my life that's unforgiven. Expose it, and cleanse me, Oh Lord."

Verse 8: *Let me hear joy and gladness; let the bones you have crushed rejoice.* "But don't stop there. Let me feel your peace. Let me feel the joy of being forgiven. Let me rejoice in being right with you. Let me know I am free from all sin and right with you, O God. Give me the peace that comes from knowing I am forgiven. For then, I can rejoice with gladness."

Verse 9: *Hide your face from my sins and blot out all my iniquity.* "Refuse to see my sins any longer or I will die. If you don't blot **all** of my iniquity, I will miss eternity with you. That I cannot bear. Blot **all** of my iniquity, not just today's or yesterday's sin. Recall **all** my sins no more. Hide my **every** sin so You never see them again."

Verse 10: *Create in me a pure heart, O God, and renew a steadfast spirit within me.* "I know I don't deserve your attention, but still, I ask for a heart that only You can give. Don't just purify my heart, also make my spirit strong and firm so I remain faithful to you. Do what is required to increase my faith. Help me live my daily life dependent on You, Oh God."

Verse 11: *Do not cast me from your presence or take your Holy Spirit from me.* "I know I deserve to be tossed away from your presence, but still, I plead for the comfort Your Holy

Spirit can provide. Let Him stay with me and guide me as I go forward. I need His help for such help is the only way this depraved heart of mine can change and remain faithful. I want to live for you, Lord, and I know I can only do that with Your help."

Verse 12: **Restore to me the joy of your salvation and grant me a willing spirit to sustain me.** "Only with Your pardon and full forgiveness can I know I still receive Your salvation, and knowing this, is all that can give me joy. While I have wandered away from You, I have not forgotten how joyful it is to know Your goodness and grace. Give me a strong willfulness to remain faithful."

Verse 13: **Then I will teach transgressors your ways and sinners will turn back to you.** "Joyful of your forgiveness, I will use what I have learned from my sin, confession, and Your faithful forgiveness, to help others who are trapped in sin as I was. I will share how great is Your love and forgiveness so others will repent, accept Your pardon, and glorify Your greatness."

Verse 14: **Save me from bloodguilt, O God, the God who saves me, and my tongue will sing of your righteousness.** "I know Your Law proves I am deserving of death. But if You choose to save me, I will sing of Your righteousness so all can hear. I will be glad and filled with joy, I will sing of Your righteous love."

Verse 15: *O Lord, open my lips, and my mouth will declare your praise.* "Unlock my lips. Stop my feelings of shame and guilt so my lips can declare your praises again. Let Your goodness and forgiveness be something I cannot keep quiet. Let me shout of your goodness."

Verse 16: *You do not delight in sacrifice or I would bring it; you do not take pleasure in burnt offerings.* "I now understand what it is You want from me, and I will gladly give the sacrifice You desire. You don't want the sacrificial blood of an animal; You want my heart and a willingness to repent when I do wrong. I give you that, O God."

Verse: 17: *The sacrifices of God are a broken spirit; a broken and contrite heart, O GOD, You will not despise.* "The sacrifice You want is to know man is heartbroken over his every sin. You want to know my guilt overwhelms me so I will change and be faithful to You. To love You is to repent and plead for Your help to remain faithful, and this I do. My broken heart is what You desire, not my arrogant, self-righteous heart that has me thinking my sin is minor or unimportant. You want me to confess my weaknesses and let You heal me. This is what I will sing aloud because it's what ensures eternity with You."

David's prayer proved his heart and conscience were soft and pliable. We can expect God to guide us if we meet with Him in prayer as David did. However, we are cautioned that **sin can become a progressive addiction, with an unsatisfied lust for more** (Eph. 4:19 my emphasis). As David's prayer shows, praying keeps one's heart moldable by the Lord. It is why God's forgiveness and promise to recall our sins no more is such a monumental blessing.

Repentance indicates our sorrow for having done wrong by God's standard and shows a commitment to change. Remember, no matter our sin, Jesus said we sin because we don't love Him, don't love His Word, and despise His oath. No matter what type of sin we commit., the real guilt is that every sin shows we are doing things our way instead of living the Lord's way, so even a little white lie is deadly serious to Him and says we aren't loving Him. The smallest most insignificant sin by our standards still hurts the Lord and proves what rebellious hearts we have. It shows how we are like the stubborn Israelites. Remember, Jesus said, *"If you love me, you will obey what I command"* (Jn. 14:15).

Lest this leaves one thinking that all we pray about is our sinfulness, let me suggest that we can pray many times to do nothing but thank the Lord for our blessings, or pray for others, or pray without asking for anything, or pray without even knowing what we need. During such times the Lord responds because He knows we are reaching for Him.

Let me share such an example that is personal, a time when I faced a really dark period in my life. One of my lowest. My family was miles away, with no way to see them for some time. I was missing my children terribly, and things at work were trying. The place where I worked was closing. I had to relocate hundreds of miles away or face unemployment. As I drove out of the company's parking lot, the sky was as black as I felt. The closer I got to home, the heavier and darker the clouds grew. Just before I pulled into the garage, rain pounded my windshield so hard I could barely see. I opened the back door to a cold, dark, empty house and realized I was hungry. I had not eaten all day. I don't like breakfast, and a noon meeting dragged on too long. Opening the refrigerator, I stared at the shelves for several minutes. Nothing looked good, and I was too depleted to cook. I closed the door and dropped to the floor. Tears streamed down my cheeks. I could not stop crying. I sat muttering *"Holy Father, I am so miserable."* Sitting in the floor, I repeated the same words several times. Then the telephone interrupted. I stood up and grabbed the receiver to hear my friend, Mardale, say, *"This is really strange. We are only having soup beans, corn bread, and salad for dinner, but I want you to come eat with us. And I just have to tell you this: Bud and I were in the back yard picking up leaves and sticks, trying to finish before it rained. I told him that I didn't know why, but I felt such a strange feeling I had to stop right then and phone you. Bud asked me to help finish first, but I told him I couldn't, that I had to call you right now. It could not wait. I literally ran into the house to call you."* I will always believe it was the Holy Spirit telling Mardale to help me.

I understood David saying, *"You know when I sit and when I rise; you perceive my thoughts from afar. Before a word is on my tongue, you know it completely, O LORD"* (Ps. 139: 2, 4). That evening I had not said what most consider a prayer. I couldn't. I was to overcome with sorrow and stress to know how. All I could do was take my heart to God with His name and repeat the same words again and again. I asked for nothing. Thanked Him for nothing. I only repeated His name, but the anguish of my heart showed my pain and need, and I believed the Lord was present. I had sought God's help in my moment of distress. My prayer proved that He answers even the tiniest, mustard-seed-size prayer. And He responded in a way that helped tremendously so I would know Jesus and the Holy Spirit had intervened and carried my words to the Father.

I believe we give God glory by laying our needs before His holy throne instead of trying to wrestle with pain on our own. He knew I didn't need to be alone that evening. If I had been, I wouldn't have eaten. God showed me He was present, and He gave me time with friends to eat the most appreciated meal I may have ever enjoyed. Leaving them, I was able to go home to a restful sleep.

Just think, at any time, we can talk to the Father and to the Lord Jesus who spoke our universe into existence. He welcomes us into His presence. In fact, we are urged to *come boldly to the throne of grace, that we may obtain mercy and find grace to help in time of need.* (Heb. 4:16). I knew a Christian needed to have a mind-set of prayer, and those few words were all I knew to say. Yet, they proved all I needed to say because God so wants to stay in close relationship with us.

While prayers are often more meaningful during quiet times alone with the Lord, even amid crowds, we can pray inside our thoughts, the closet of our minds. Remember, Jesus knows our thoughts (Mt. 9:4;12:25; Lk. 5:22; 11:17). Anytime and anyplace, we can pray and know He listens and is eager to care for us.

Prayer clears human obstacles out of the way in order for our Father to work. Certainly, the Father can work without our prayers, but He made prayer a part of His plan for accomplishing His will in this world. As C. S. Lewis is noted to have said, *"God is the fuel that our spirits were designed to burn. There is no other."*

AT OUR MOMENT OF DEATH

W here I worshiped years ago, a woman who had recently lost her husband asked the elders to help her pray to die. She had no children, could no longer drive, struggled to walk, and felt a burden to the Church's women on whom she depended for care. She believed she was heaven-bound and wanted to go live with the Lord. The elders announced her wish at the following service and asked others to pray with her. Within a month, we celebrated her powerful faith at her funeral. *Precious in the sight of the Lord is the death of His saints* (Ps. 117:15).

Some are surprised to learn that many true believers find comfort and peace in facing death. In fact, many Christians, especially the elderly and terminally ill, pray to die. Our bodies were made so they experience pain and groan to be clothed with a heavenly dwelling (2 Cor. 5:4). They are longing for a better home –a heavenly one. *Therefore, God is not ashamed to be called their God, for He has prepared a city for them* (Heb. 11:16). Leaving loved ones may disturb them, but it does not discourage them. For a faithful believer, to live is Christ, but **to die is gain** (Phil. 1:21). The foundation of their faith gives them the comfort of knowing that with death they will be with the Lord and their faithful loved ones for eternity in a place that's better than here. Such was David's confidence: *I am confident of this: I will see the goodness of the LORD in the land of the living* (Ps. 27:13). Those who pray to die, do not fear death; they yearn for heaven.

Often, we don't understand when someone young dies, but Scriptures tells us that *the righteous are taken away to be spared from evil* (Isa. 57:1). God is in control and caring for them. He assures us they enter into peace and find rest as they lie in death (v.2). How long we live is ordained and written in God's Book before we are born (Ps. 139:16).

Death separates man's soul from his body. Man is an soul that lives inside a body that's subjected to decay. The soul is what lives after one's death (Ps 116:8). Solomon described death as being the moment when the breath of man returns to God who gave it (Ecc. 12:7), the One who during creation breathed into man's nostrils the breath of life, so man became a living being (Ge. 2:7; Ps. 104:30). When man dies, God takes away man's spirit and the breath returns to God (Ecc. 12:7). Note spirit and breath are often used interchangeably, and neither describe or substitute for the soul.

Man was given a human body that is wrapped around his soul. With death, the body decays, but the soul was created to live forever. Each soul will be given a new body when Jesus returns. Then the soul with its new indestructible body will either live forever in Paradise with the Lord or in hell for eternity. The soul is the part of man that is eternally impacted by his character and morals, while the spirit is what others recognize. For example, we know when a ball team takes the field fired up, determined to win, and gives 100%. We say, *"Boy, they have team spirit today."* We have all watched a child who keeps grabbing candy as his mother tries to pay for groceries. No matter how many times she takes the candy from him, he grabs it again, screaming. The child has a strong self-will and rebellious spirit. Both the team and child displayed an excited, enthusiastic breath (spirit) that's driven by the values they hold in their hearts. Our spirit is an inner force we can control with self-will by asking, *"If I do this, what does it show I am valuing?* What our heart values drives the choices we make and is shown in how we behave. For example, the Israelites disobeyed, while *Caleb had a different spirit, and followed the Lord wholeheartedly,* and he was blessed by God (Nu. 14:24). Caleb's heart valued serving the Lord and such a spirit ensured his soul was heaven-bound while many Israelites' spirits guaranteed their souls were not.

Two things last forever. One is the truth of God's word and the souls of men (Mk. 13:31). The soul differs from the heart (Dt. 26:16; 30:6), and from the spirit and mind (Mt. 22:37; Mk 12:30: Lk. 10:27). We protect our souls with a spirit that values the truth of God's word and listening to the Holy

Spirit's help (1 Pe. 1:22). Jesus is the Shepherd of our souls (! Pe. 2:25). David describes Jesus as having a soul (Ps. 16:9-10).

At one's death, the body goes to the grave, and the faithful believer's soul goes to meet the Lord. While the body sleeps in its grave, the soul enters into the presence of the Lord (Phil 1:23-24; 2 Cor. 5:6-8) and rests from its labors (Rev. 14:3). The soul who lives committing willful sins is the one who is dead to the blessing of heaven and lives in hell (the second death) (Eze. 18:4). The soul that lives striving to be faithful lives eternally with the holy Godhead (Ps. 116:8). The word of God divides soul and spirit, judging men's hearts that are laid bare before the eyes of Him to whom we must give account (Heb. 4: 12-13).

As faithful believers' souls are freed from their earthly bodies, they are met by ministering angels sent to carry them into Jesus Christ's glorious presence. Such is the example in the story of Lazarus, the beggar, and the rich man (Lk. 16: 19-31 my emphasis). *The time came when the beggar died and **the angels carried him to Abraham's side.*** The angels carried the beggar through the stary sky to the third heaven where Jesus Christ, the Son of man, entered to live in Paradise. *The highest heaven belongs to the Lord; earth He has given to man* (Ps. 115:16). Imagine being in a place so wonderful that the Holy Spirit had men writing the Bible call it Paradise.

However, the rich man also died and was buried. In Hell, his soul was in torment, but he could see Abraham and Lazarus. Note that he waited in hell for Judgment Day. Yet, he was able to see where he could have been spending eternity but was now unable to go (2 Cor. 12:2-4; Lk.23:43). What torment it will be to live in constant suffering while seeing Paradise for eternity without being able to enter. Death ends all hope of change.

It is no different today. Let me share a mini-version of a true event I included in my book, *God Wants to Say Yes*. It is about Davy, a five-year-old boy who lay dying with rapidly spreading brain cancer. His parents moved to live with his grandparents so they could share having someone continually sitting beside Davy. At first, Davy complained of pain, but little by little he became more like a vegetable. He lost his hearing, then his sight, and eventually was unable to swallow. At that point he stopped speaking and rarely opened his eyes. Then early one morning as his grandmother was washing his face and singing to him, he opened his eyes. Almost yelling Davy said, *"They're coming Grams. I see them!"*

"Who, honey? Who's coming?" she asked in surprise.

"Jesus! I see the angels!" With these words, Davy shut his eyes, never to open them again until arriving in Paradise with the Lord and being comforted in Abraham's bosom.

I asked my student who shared this personal experience if his family attended worship. He said they randomly did before Davy died, but now they never miss a worship service because Davy's experience increased their faith and assurance of heaven. I reminded him, *"Sometimes, God uses the most unbearably painful situation for our eternal good. What a blessing that you can spend eternity with Davy and never again be separated."*

Just as angels accompanied Davy to Paradise, they protect the souls of the faithful from any spiritual warfare as they cross the spiritual realm to reach Abraham's side of the fixed chasm that separates Paradise from Hell/ Hades (Lk. 16:22). Webster defines chasm as a deep abyss, and Scripture says angels ensure the faithful are carried safely across it (Lk. 16:22). God fixed the deep chasm so no one from either side can cross over to the other side (Lk. 16: 26). Souls in hell have no hope of ever going to heaven. They postponed too long their need to change.

Souls of the faithful are carried to Paradise, a place where they are comforted (v. 25). It is the place Jesus promised to meet – that very day – with the thief on the cross who acknowledged Jesus' divinity, because *even in death the righteous have a refuge* (Prov. 4:32). It was the other thief who was transported to Hades. Hades is a horrid place where the unfaithful dead agonize in fire and sulfur as they await their final judgment (Lk. 16: 24).

Because Paradise is where believers belong, they meet with Jesus, our permanent high priest, who is able to **save completely those who come to God through Him** (Heb. 7:24-25 my emphasis). And be with Him, who, after His resurrection, ascended higher than all the heavens in order to fill the whole universe (Eph. 4:10).

The moment a faithful believer stops breathing, his soul goes to meet with Jesus Christ in Paradise, a place immeasurably better than anything here (Phil. 1:23). The physical body remains in the grave until Jesus returns for the Judgment and unites all men's souls with new imperishable bodies (Rev. 32:1). We received new bodies because flesh and blood cannot inherit the kingdom of God (1 Th. 4:16; 2 Cor. 5:6). In heaven, mankind awaits the judgment by singing and praising God (Rev. 14:1-4). Their souls are raised in glory (2 Cor. 5:1-4), and will see Him just as He is (1 Jn. 3:2), because eternal life is to know the true God (Father) and Jesus Christ (Jn. 17:3). There will be no more wondering what God is really like because they now delight in the presence of His overwhelming glory (Rev. 4:1-11).

The Savior will rejoice when He receives the souls He loved and planned for before the beginning of this world. No one will be happier for their arrival than Jesus Christ. Their arrival completes Christ's joy that enabled Him to endure the cross, with the contempt of its shame; all for mankind's sake (Heb. 12:2). Christ could tolerate the suffering of the cross, knowing it would allow the faithful to live forever in heaven with Him. That's how much He loves His faithful ones.

Jesus will spread His tent over the souls in heaven so they will never hunger, thirst, or be scorched by heat. The Lamb of God will be their Good Shepherd and lead them to springs of living water. He will wipe away every tear from their eyes (Rev. 7:14-17). He will dwell with them: they will be His people, and He will be their God. There will be no more death, or mourning, or crying, or pain. For them, **the old order of things has passed away** (Rev. 21:3-4 my emphasis).

Upon arrival in Paradise, one's soul will be met with great rejoicing by those who were already there. These believers have passed from death to life (Jn. 5:24), a permanent eternal life. Their arrival ensures Satan can never again tempt them, and they're forever freed from an environment filled with sin, sorrow, and sickness. No more will they suffer, or hurt, or feel sad. Their souls arrive wearing white robes, because they were washed pure in the blood of the Lamb with baptism. The souls will serve the Lord Jesus in His temple, and He will sit on His throne with them (Rev. 7:15, Rev. 4:1-11). They will glorify and praise Jesus for the price He paid to make eternity with Him possible.

We can only imagine the many stories these souls share with each other as they delight in reunions. What freedom and comfort they will enjoy as they interact with others who will never hurt them and with whom they will never cause any discomfort, because all interactions will demonstrate genuine love.

How prized it will be for the saved to sit in heaven recalling how the Lord had protected them, guided them, and tested them when they needed their faith strengthened. They will now grasp the meaning of things they didn't understand at the time, and realize the many times the Lord kept them going when they were too weak to go alone. How thankful these faithful souls will be that He saved them from the dangers and pitfalls where they could have been lost forever.

The souls in heaven will rejoice in the Father's love that He had for them before the foundation of the world and for being granted His saving grace. They will cherish the ways the Holy Spirit pushed and nudged them to keep them on track and kept pressing them to grow spiritually. They will finally realize the many ways that Jesus worked all things for their eternal good (Ro. 8:28).

They will realize how Christ worked in His Church. They will delight as the Churches of Christ flourish on earth, and how the Lord's purposes are fulfilled in His Church's work. Now these souls can share in heaven's joyful celebration when another prodigal sinner decides to return home to remain faithful to the Lord. Imagine a Grandmother's joy when she knows her grandchild has come back home. The souls can listen as Abraham, Moses, and David explain how their Covenants unfolded and helped to bring about the Lord's Church with its many victories and trials throughout the world. They will meet the many martyrs who were persecuted because of their faith in Christ, and who are now blessed with a white robe (Rev. 6: 9-11). Most of all, they will rejoice that the offer of salvation was given to both Jews and Gentiles in order to save the entire world. They will finally comprehend how all are one in the Lord.

These blessed souls will dwell with Jesus in a state of perfect rest as John was told in Revelation (14:13 my emphasis): *"Blessed are the dead who die in the Lord from now on." "Yes," says the Spirit, "They will rest from their labor, for **their deeds will follow them.**"* They remain in a state of great joy, awaiting the Judgment. The souls in heaven have no fear of Judgment Day. They have no sins to be publicly announced because they believed that Jesus paid the price for all their sins, were baptized, and intercedes for them with every repentance. They over-flow with happiness because no matter how bad their repented sins, the Father remembers their sins no more.

For a description of heaven read Ezekiel (1:1-28) and John's account in Revelation. Their images are beyond anything we have on earth to compare. Still, we can envision jewels, colored lights, and angelic beings all flashing and displaying a beautiful brilliance. Both men describe a place with the intense glory of God and His love being poured on His holy family of believers.

The second coming of Jesus Christ to earth is to take for Himself people who are His very own, and who are eager to do what is good (Ti. 2:14). Until then, they rest in Him, knowing He will keep His promise, and He will return to judge all on earth in His Father's own set time.

No one but the Father knows when Jesus will return to earth, not Jesus nor the angels (Mt. 24:36). However, we do know the Father has appointed a time for the Judgment of all, and **the Son of Man will come at an hour when no one is expecting Him** (v. 44 my emphasis). Unexpectedly, His return will occur so fast, people will be shocked, for it will happen in the twinkle of an eye. There will be no time for sinful men to change (1 Cor. 15:52). The Son of Man's coming will be like the lightening, which flashes and lights up the sky from one end to the other. People will be busy going about their daily activities, as they were in Noah's day when the rain came and destroyed them all (Lk. 17:23-26). But all will see Him.

Just as the unbelieving have yet to face their judgment and full punishment, so have the faithful not yet appeared before the judgment seat of Christ. Paul told believers in Corinth that **whether we are at home in the body or away from it, we must all appear before the judgment seat of Christ**. It is so each one may receive what is due him for the things done while in the body, whether good or bad (2 Cor. 5:10 my emphasis). The faithful will be rewarded for all their good deeds. Whoever believes in Him is not condemned. Whoever does not believe stands condemned already, because he has not believed in God's One and Only Son (Jn. 3:17-18).

The unbelieving will know their reasons for being sent to hell, and no one will argue with the Lord that day. The time for communicating and pleading with Him will be over. Anyone who thinks they will be given an opportunity to defend their disobedience, needs to read God's answer to Job who thought he could question the Lord (Job 38-42). God asked Job, *"Will the one who contends with the Almighty correct Him?"* Standing in the Lord's presence ensures man knows how sinful he is and how holy and righteous Jesus is. One of man's greatest failures is his failing to fully grasp how far superior God is to us in every way. His thoughts and ways are higher than ours and are nothing like ours (Isa. 55:8-9). As Job answered the Lord so will such people, *"I am unworthy – how can I reply to you? I put my hand over my mouth. I will say no more"* (Job 40:4-5). And so, it will be with the condemned on Judgment Day.

One of man's greatest failures is his failing to fully grasp how far superior God is to us in every way

Believers with faith like Noah, who built an ark with holy fear and became an heir of righteousness, await with excitement the rewards Jesus brings with Him when He returns to judge the world (Eph.6:8). For them, the Judgment Seat of Christ has to do with how believers lived for Christ after He saved them. They stand before Jesus to receive their reward. *Behold, I am coming soon!* **My reward is with me,** *and I will give to everyone according to what he has done (Rev. 22:12).* Everything believers have done for Christ will be evaluated and rewarded (Gen 15:1; Isa. 40:10; Mt. 6:4, 8, 18; 10;42; Lk 6: 23, 35; Eph. 6:8; Heb. 10:35; 11:6). He who is kind to the poor lends to the LORD, and He will reward him for what he has done (Prov. 19:17). Surely, the very best reward is being adopted as a child of God the Father and heir and brother of Jesus, knowing we are forever a full member of the family in heaven (Eph. 1:5; Ro. 8:23; Gal.4:7). As Jesus said, *"For my Father's will is that everyone who looks to the Son and believes in Him shall have eternal life, and I will raise him up at the last day"* (Jn. 6:40). *If God is for us, who can be against us? He who did not spare His own Son, but* **gave Him up for us** __all__ *– how* **will** *He not also along with Him,* **graciously give us all things?** *(Ro. 8:31-32* my emphasis). Christ took away the sins of many people, and He will appear a second time, not to bear our sins but to bring salvation to the faithful who are waiting for Him (Heb. 9:28).

God did not send His Son into the world to condemn the world, but to save the world through Him. Jesus will be the judge at the Father's appointed Day of Judgement. However, until Jesus returns, His duty is not to judge people but to continue serving as **the Way every person can be saved**. Still, at the Father's chosen time, Jesus is coming with thousands upon thousands of His holy ones to judge everyone (Jude 1:14).

How wonderful to know that the faithful have nothing to fear on that Day, because Jesus will be their advocate. He has compassion for our every struggle because He experienced abuse, temptation, and rejection while on earth. He serves as our High Priest and defends those who have lived trying to remain faithful but still sin (1 Jn. 1:1-2; Heb. 4:1`5, 9:28). The many sins the faithful are thankful others don't know about will not be announced that Day, because our guilt and the Holy Spirit's prodding ensured we confessed these wrongs, and the Father has no memory of them. A special favor is that we will no longer remember negative times we experienced while on earth.

For the first four weeks after my husband died, I could not function. I have no memory of eating or of even getting dressed. I did nothing but sit in a recliner thinking about the good times we had shared and crying for the future plans we had made that would now never be. We had a good relationship. We rarely argued. We laughed and hugged often. When asked a question, we couldn't believe how we both immediately had the same answers. We teased about how, maybe, we had overdone the goal of oneness and thought too much alike.

However, the seventh week after his death, I spent a day recalling a disagreement we had 25 or 30 years ago. He had decided to buy me an expensive mixer, and I didn't want it enough to spend so much money. Despite my repeated protest, he purchased it. I was upset for a quite a while for being unable to influence him about something that only I would use. Now I realized this bothered me more than the cost of the mixer. And today, I could not remember apologizing or even later thanking him for the mixer that I have enjoyed for years. Anytime he and I had a disagreement that lasted longer than it should, he always apologized. Now recalling the situation, I was bothered that maybe I hadn't. I cried, and prayed, and cried some more. I asked God to forgive me and to have my husband forgive me. Then I realized, my husband no longer has such a memory. Now with the Lord, if he does remember his time on earth, it will be only our best of times. In heaven there is no crying or sadness, and not even a twinge of prior hurt feelings. For him, all is peaceful and gladness.

How happy I was once I realized he would not remember the situation even if I had failed to say I was sorry. So, I asked God to forgive me for how I had behaved. Then I let it go. I had to let our shared past be as it was, and someway learn to grieve for the future plans I had anticipated with him but now would never be. I had to create a different present, not continue clinging to unfulfilled expectations.

God's New Covenant promises will prove better and more wonderful than anything the saints who arrive in heaven could have dreamed or imagined. And I value the day I realized God's Covenant promise also has a blessing for those of us left behind when our loved ones go to heaven. We can be tempted to focus on particular negative events, and let them override the good memories. Then I realized that all negative times with our departed loved ones are gone forever. Our loved ones in heaven cannot recall them, and we have no reason to. We can let go of all guilt, and blame, and wounds of the past, and no longer be burdened by them. What a special blessing! It frees us to engage in life today and fill it by doing whatever good we can in the present.

I have loved ones I want to see again and how nice knowing we will never disagree, argue, or cause each other any hurt. How wonderful that sounds. And yes, God really does give those of us left behind a blessing of peace.

JUDGEMENT DAY

R ecently, a Facebook friend posted a note requesting ideas for discussing with her father, who had weeks to live, his need to accept Jesus as his Lord and Savior. While she received many ideas, the type faithful believers might suggest, she received one very different comment. This unique suggestion was for her not to worry if her dad wasn't saved. She said, *"Because he was a good man, God would definitely want him in heaven"*. This woman's response revealed how little Scripture some people know.

Heaven is not a gift we gain by finding someone who will testify we were a good person. None of us are good enough, nor do enough good deeds to deserve being in the holy Godhead's presence. None of us have pure hearts. Our inner beings are tainted with sin. Jesus will not judge you based on my opinion of you, nor judge me by your idea of me. We are judged by Jesus' standard, and even when we strive to be faithful, we continually fall short. Thank God for His loving grace and for Jesus being our advocate with the Father.

When it is time for the Judgment, *God (Father) will bring with Jesus those who have fallen asleep in Him* and are currently with Him in Paradise. Jesus will return in flaming fire with

His mighty angels to judge the world. His return will surprise people for He will come like a thief (2 Pe. 3:9). No one will avoid Him. Every eye will see Him, even those who pierced Him; and all the peoples of the earth will morn because of Him (Rev. 1:7).

When one dies, the soul goes to be with Jesus, and the perishable earthly body is sown in weakness. But when the trumpet sounds marking Jesus' return, multitudes of bodies who slept in the dust of the earth will be awakened, the sea will give up the dead, as will those who were being held in Hades (Dan. 12:2). All in their graves will hear His voice and come out – those who have done good will rise to live and those who have done evil will rise to be condemned (Jn. 5:29). Jesus will raise man's natural body as a new spiritual body that is imperishable. The new bodies will bear the likeness of Jesus' resurrected body (1 Cor. 15: 42-49). After being judged, all will either permanently enjoy heaven or forever suffer in hell with a soul that has a new body that is imperishable.

Those who are still alive, who are left till the coming of the Lord, will certainly not precede those who have fallen asleep. For the Lord Himself will come down from heaven with a loud command, with the voice of the archangel, and with the trumpet call of God. The dead in Christ will rise first. After that, we who are still alive and are left will be caught up together with them in the clouds to meet the Lord in the air. And so, we will be with the Lord forever (1 Th. 4:14-17).

When the saved, who are still alive, view the glory of Jesus descending on earth with the holy angels, and the souls who have been residing with Him in heaven, what a special display it will be for them to see! The saved will be thrilled because it means once the judgment is over, heaven is theirs, and they are forever freed of earth's trials, demands, and sorrows. All the injustice in this world will cease.

However, Jesus' appearance will put terror in the wicked because it will be too late to repent and be baptized. They will never again hear the gospel preached or have time to change. Their eternal fate will be sealed forever.

On Judgment Day, Jesus' fire will radiate the brilliance of His glory as He gathers the saved and brings a terrible, fiery punishment for the unsaved. Jesus will dispense the Father's righteous anger against sin, just as Moses destroyed all the people who begged Aaron to make a golden calf and worshipped it.

Judgment Day has to include fire because fire is part of Jesus' nature. Just as love, forgiveness, and mercy are attributes of the Lord, so are judgment and fire. Scripture calls Jesus a consuming fire, not that He creates fire, but rather, it's a fire with a brilliant glow that displays His holiness. Jesus' eyes are like a blazing fire (Rev. 1:14, 19:12), and His feet are like bronze glowing in a furnace (Rev. 1:15). Blazing with fire can be no other way for the One who hates sins and has paid such a monumental price so all people of all times and in all places could be forgiven and saved. I used to wonder how our human eyes could handle such brilliance until remembering we will have an indestructible body with eyes that can't be hurt.

Jesus will reward those who have lived striving to be good and helping others in need, and He will punish the stubbornly sinful. When He said we must be born again (baptized), He meant it, for it proves we believe Jesus is God's Son who died so His blood could pay for our sins. Jesus has never forgiven disobedience at the expense of His holiness, nor will that change on Judgment Day. His justice is absolute. His demand of moral purity unbending. Until then, He remains eager to forgive and forget the wrongs of even the worst, wicked sinners who change. It's is why He paid the price required for their forgiveness with His own unbearable suffering in death. But His love for righteousness won't let Him excuse willful and continued rebellion. He must judge all, the good and the bad.

Jesus will sit on His throne in heavenly glory with all nations gathered before Him. He will separate the people one from another, as a shepherd separates the sheep from the goats. He will put the sheep on His right and the goats on His left. Each person will be judged.

The dead, great and small, will stand before the throne and the books opened, one being the Book of Life and another His Scroll of Remembrance. Jesus sees how we behave today towards others and records our words and actions in His books. He saves our record until Judgment Day (Mal. 3:16; Rev. 21:12-13). Good deeds go in as our permanent deposit because He created us to do good works (Eph. 2:10). When we help others He takes it personal, as if we had done it for Him. *He who is kind to the poor lends to the LORD, and He will reward him for what he has done* (Prov. 19:17).

Those whose names are written in the Lamb's (Jesus') Book of Life will see heaven (Rev. 21:27). Nothing impure will enter heaven, nor will anyone who does what is hateful or deceitful, but only those whose names are written in the Lamb's Book of Life (Rev. 21:26). Anyone's name not found in His Book will be separated, with the disobedient going to eternal punishment (Rev. 20:12).

In Jesus' Judgment, there will be no miscarriage of justice. Jesus is a righteous judge (Ps. 7:11; 2 Ti. 4:8), and a just judge (Jn. 5:30). The Father will bring every secret thing we have done into judgment through Jesus Christ (Ro. 2:16). The condemned cannot plead their case or argue with His decision, because He knows all our thoughts, deeds, words, and motives (1 Cor. 4:4). *A man's ways are in full view of the Lord, and He examines all his paths* (Prov. 5:21). He weighs man's motives (Prov. 16:2). Jesus will bring to light the hidden things of darkness that people have done, and He reveals the counsels of their hearts (1 Cor. 4:5). Those whose words and actions show God's law was written in their hearts (by moral living) have consciences that bear witness and confirm it. One's thoughts will either accuse them or excuse them (Ro. 2:15). Jesus will judge them without partiality (Co. 3:25). No one will be mistakenly rewarded heaven or wrongly condemned to hell.

To the sheep on His right, Jesus will say, "*Come, you who are blessed by my Father; take your inheritance, the kingdom prepared for you since the creation of the world*" (Mt. 25:34). Because Jesus' blood covers all their sins, they have no sins to be announced. As Colossians (1:22-23) reveals, those who continued in their faith and held to their hope are reconciled to the Father by Christ's blood shed for us. Christ will present them as holy in His sight, without blemish and free from accusation. The righteous will be forever rewarded with bountiful blessings in Paradise because there is no condemnation for those who are in Christ Jesus. Those who proved they were trying to live for Him will receive praise from God (1 Cor. 4:5), and any added reward each faithful believer receives determined.

All works and deeds that believers did while on earth will be tested by God, and those that are worthy will be rewarded. *Behold, I am coming soon!* **My reward is with me**, *and I will give to everyone according to what he has done* (Rev. 22:12 my emphasis).

However, our eternal salvation is not won by good works. We inherit heaven by God's grace because of our faith and baptismal birthright. All obedient born-again believer's inheritance is secure. *At the end of your days,* **you will rise to receive your allotted inheritance** (Dan. 12:13 my emphasis). These are the Father's adopted children and Jesus' siblings who inherit all things (Rev. 21:7; Mk. 3:34; Heb. 2:11; Ro. 8:29). Faithful believers will be saved, and their good deeds rewarded (Rev. 2:7; 3:21). *I the LORD search the heart and examine the mind, to* **reward** *a man according to his conduct, according to* **what his deeds deserve** (Jer. 17:10 my emphasis).

One's entrance into heaven is guaranteed by acceptance of Jesus Christ's sacrifice and God's grace. But all of our works and deeds, no matter how good we may have thought they were, will not be rewarded. Some of our works have no eternal value. *Fire will test the quality of each man's work.* Some of our good deeds required deep sacrifice and effort with a purpose of glorifying the Father. These are surely worth their weight in gold or silver. Other deeds have little or no value and are of no more worth than paper or stubble and will be burned away. Jesus is going to reward our motives and sacrifices that glorified the Father. *If what he has built survives, he will receive his reward. If it is burned up, he will suffer loss;* **he himself will be saved**, *but only as one escaping through the flames* (1 Cor. 3:13-15 my emphasis). While good deeds do not all receive the same rewards, the baptized who remain faithful are declared perfect, and they have no fear of condemnation (1 Cor. Ro. 5:1; 8:1). Heaven is theirs!

Those who were wise will shine like the brightness of the heavens, just as those who led many to righteousness will glow like the stars forever and ever (Dan. 12:3). What eternal happiness there will be for those in heaven, knowing the Godhead personally and intimately. The faithful elderly who prayed to go onto heaven are thankful they chose to get to be with the Lord sooner and longer.

However, the goats on Jesus' left will hear depart from Me, you who are cursed into the eternal fire prepared for the devil and his angels. For when I was hungry you gave Me nothing to eat and did not clothe Me, nor did you look after Me when I was sick. What you did not do for the least ones, you did not do for Me. Jesus takes how we help others personal. A crucial factor in being rewarded heaven is having our names recorded in God's Scroll of Remembrance for fearing Him and honoring His name (Mal. 3:16), and in His Book of Life that shows we loved the Lord and offered needed care to others (Phil 4:3; Rev. 3:4; Prov. 14:31). Those who loved others enough to be moved to helpful actions will be rewarded, because they saw it as glorifying God to help people whom He loved. However, those who failed to show mercy to others will receive no mercy from the Lord on that Day (Js. 2:13).

Death and Hades will be thrown into the lake of fire, the second death, as will everyone whose names are not found written in God's Book of Life (Rev. 20:11-15). What eternal screams, groans, and tears will be shed among those in Hell. The doomed cannot protest because Jesus was the most prolific teacher about hell in the Bible. He spoke more about repentance and hell than heaven. Everyone could have known.

Jesus said, *"Out of the heart, the mouth speaks. Men will have to give account on the Day of Judgment for every careless word they have spoken. For by your words, you will be acquitted, and by your words you will be condemned"* (Mt. 12:34-37). *"There is a judge for the one who rejects Me and who does not accept My words; that very* *word which I spoke will condemn him at the last day. For I did not speak of My own accord, but **the Father** who sent me **commanded Me what to say and how to say it**"* (Jn. 12:48-50 my emphasis). The dead are judged by things written in God's Books. They will be separated, with the unbelieving going to eternal punishment, and righteous believers to eternal life (Mt. 25:34-46).

Sinners should tremble at the thought of God's impending judgment. As Hebrews (10:31) states, *it is a dreadful thing to fall into the hands of the living God.* Because at that point, there are no second chances to escape Hell, and there can be no sin in heaven. Their fate is irreversible and lasts throughout eternity because their souls with new bodies are now indestructible.

Today, the Father makes the sun to rise on the evil and the good, and sends rain on the righteous and unrighteous (Mt. 5:45). But after the judgement, the wicked will be eternally separated from God, from all His blessings, and from righteous believers. *"This will happen when the Lord Jesus is revealed from heaven in blazing fire with His powerful angels. He will punish those who do not know God and do not obey the gospel of your Lord Jesus. They will be punished with everlasting destruction and **shut out from the presence of the Lord and from the majesty of His power** on the day He comes to be glorified in His holy people and to be marveled at among all those who have* *believed"* (2 Thes. 1:7-10). The condemned will know only weeping and gnashing of teeth without any hope of ever having anything better. On them will rain fiery coals and burning sulfur. A scorching wind will be their lot (Ps. 11:6). As Charles Spurgeon is noted for saying, *"To have a body in hell, with all of its sinful desires, but not have the power to satisfy them, how horrible hell will be!"*

Many will mourn Jesus' return more than others because the Bible describes more people going to hell than heaven and some in hell and receiving a sterner, more painful punishment (Mt. 10:15; 11:21-24; Lk 12: 47-48; Heb. 10:29; 2 Pe. 2:10-21; Rev. 20:10-15). However, just because another suffers more, it does not mean the lesser punishment is bearable. All men will reap what they have sown. Certainly, the one with the least degree of punishment cannot compare to the blissful joy of someone in heaven.

They cannot blame God for their eternal destiny. Jesus Christ paid an unbearable price that made heaven free and welcome for everyone. People who face permanent destruction chose to turn away from the Lord's offer of heaven to sin willfully (Ro. 1:18-23). It's why all must take God's moral laws seriously.

God lets us ignore Him and even allows us to worship Him wrongly, but He will stop such people and deny them entrance to the narrow road that leads to the gate of heaven. Because He *who does what is sinful is of the devil* (I Jn. 3:8), the unforgiven will be turned back to take the wide way to face a fiery destruction and spend eternity with Satan and his wicked spirits. Jesus' genuine love demands an equally genuine justice.

Today, we can ignore Him, but those who reject His welcome call to become part of His heavenly family will be sent to the lake of fire for eternity. They will forever regret hating Jesus, hating His Word, hating His Light, despising the oath of His Covenant, and hating His instructions (2 Sam. 12:9-10; Jn. 15:18; Eze. 16:59; 2 Ki. 17:15; Ps. 50:17). They will finally know they cannot love both Jesus and their chosen sins.

Willful sinners make their choice, and Jesus will honor their decisions to love their sin and hate Him and let them continue hating Him for eternity. Surely, they will hate themselves for having tried to avoid facing Jesus' judgment by distracting themselves and hiding in today's comforts and pleasures that are only transient. They will grieve how they ignored that their time on earth was temporary, and heaven eternal.

Judgment may seem unfair but only when we measure it by worldly standards of wealth, power, good health, fame, status, and pleasure. Measure it with a spiritual standard, and we realize worldly types of rewards and pleasures are only temporarily, and how they keep us from realizing what matters eternally.

When Martha was speaking with Jesus about her deceased brother, Lazarus, she said, *"I know he will rise again in the **resurrection at the last day**"* (Jn. 11:24). Jesus answered, ***"I am the resurrection** and the life. He who believes in Me will live even though he dies, and whoever lives and believes in Me will never die"* (v.25). *"There is a judge for the one who rejects Me and does not accept my words; that very word which I spoke will condemn him **at the last day**"* (Jn. 12:48). On Judgment Day, Jesus will judge every person who has ever lived, and it will be ***our last day on this planet*** we call earth.

After the Judgment, everything we have known as our home and our planet will disappear. *The heavens will disappear with a roar; the elements will be destroyed with fire, and the earth and everything in it will be laid bare* (2 Pe. 3:7,10). But God will keep His promise. The faithful will enjoy a new heaven and a new earth, a home of righteousness where God delights in His people, and the sound of weeping and crying will be heard no more. Before people can call, God will answer them. They will be a people continually blessed by the Lord (Isa. 65:17-25; Rev. 21:1-5).

Isaiah explains that our past troubles will be forgotten and hidden from our eyes. *"For, behold, I create new heavens and a new earth: and* **the former shall not be remembered, nor come into mind***"* (65:16-17). In heaven, we will remember no more those we loved who are doomed to hell or that another caused us hurt or harm. We will not remember any prior bad experiences. All relationships will be satisfied with ones that are perfect and pleasurable in heaven. Nothing will be lacking in our new home.

However, those who today are currently suffering in Hades, awaiting Jesus' return to judge them, live worrying about others they love who they know are also headed to a fiery punishment. Likely, it required anguished suffering for them to wish for a way to have their remaining loved ones change so they don't also suffer in torment (Lk. 16: 27-28). I suggest, those in Hades will eternally suffer serious guilt if their loved ones don't change and make heaven their goal. They will remember for eternity that if they had accepted the Lord as their Savior, maybe, they could have helped their loved one be saved. This will surely increase their pain in hell.

Remember, before the beginning of the world, we were created because the Holy Godhead wanted us in heaven as part of Their family to love us forever, but They only want us if we return Their love. That's why They gave people free will to either love or reject Them. Heaven is a place of perfect holiness, and we only fit in if we have been purified with the blood of Christ and strive to live faithfully by obeying His commands (Heb. 1:3).

Our universe was designed as a temporary creation. Pretending this world is permanent and that we will live forever is Satan's lie that lets us ignore what really matters for all of eternity. Remember, Satan is the father of all lies (Jn. 8:44). His goal is to have us miss heaven by loving sin, not Jesus. Sadly, his scheme works with many. If Jesus comes tonight, is there anything He might say you have exchanged your eternal soul to have temporarily and enjoy briefly today?

Pretending this world is permanent and that we will live forever is Satan's lie that lets us ignore what really matters for all of eternity

The Lord seeks a willing heart that wants to give Him the best of all we have. He wants us to present our bodies as a living and holy sacrifice, because this is our spiritual service of worship (Ro. 12:1). When we strive to have our heart, soul, mind, and strength honor Him, we live looking forward to eternity with a sure and certain hope.

When we live certain we are going to heaven, we can endure anything we face in this life, because we know it is only temporary, and heaven will make perfect everything that's wrong in our lives today. God will make up for our failed relationships, unsuccessful careers, and serious health problems. Everything that hurts us today will be made perfect in heaven. It truly will be Paradise.

What others think of us matters little. All that counts is what Jesus thinks of us, and Jesus' sacrifice for us on the cross proved how deeply He loves us. Such love is more than we comprehend and certainly more than we deserve.

Because Jesus suffered and died to prove to you that He loves you, there is only one important question that you will ever need to answer. And it is, "Do you love Jesus?"

References

Christ last supper with His apostles: https://www.Jewish virtuallibrary.org/Passover-history.org

Different Covenants in the Bible. https://www.compellingtruth.Org./covenants-in-the-bible.html

Jewish Feast. www.setapartpeople.com/celebrate-pesach-feast-unleaven-bread

Lawson, Stephen J. *Foundations of Grace*. Ligonier Ministries. 2018.

MacArthur John. *Pattern of Prayers*. Moody Publisher, April 1, 1984.

Pew Research Center. https.//www.pewresearch.org/fact-tank/2012/12/10/laws-against-   blasphemy-apostasy-and-defamation-of-religion

Picture of Child Sacrifice. https://www.biblereading archeology.com/2016/05/13/did/the/Canaanites-sacrifice-their children.

Author: Dr. Wyveta Kirk

Dr. Kirk is a widow and mother of three adult children. In addition to writing Bible based books, she conducts programs for women. As a former college teacher, her passion is teaching and speaking. Contact: wyvetakirk@ymail.com

All of her books are available on Amazon and through all big book stores. Her books include:

Women Talk Men Walk Women insist an issue cannot be resolved unless they discuss it, but her demeanor is so emotional, he just wants to leave or bury himself in TV.

God Wants to Say YES, is Dr. Kirk's responses to a woman she met on line who was dying with cancer and asked questions about God's expectations of her/us.

Counseling an Adulterer was written in response to a minister's request, because he was seeing so many couples suffering with this sin.

Two Things Men Need More Than Sex was written in response to so many women feeling unloved by their husbands.

A Legacy of Love is Dr. Kirk's most popular fiction book. It is about a woman reared in foster care who learns about the Lord, when her attorney insists, she has to seek religious counseling before she can testify in court.

Made in the USA
Coppell, TX
08 June 2021